LANGUAGE!®

The Comprehensive Literacy Curriculum

Jane Fell Greene, Ed.D.

SOPRIS WEST™ EDUCATIONAL SERVICES
A CAMBIUM LEARNING COMPANY

BOSTON, MA • LONGMONT, CO

09 08 07 06   10 9 8 7 6 5 4 3

Editorial Director: Nancy Chapel Eberhardt
Word and Phrase Selection: Judy Fell Woods
English Learners: Jennifer Wells Greene
Lesson Development: Sheryl Ferlito, Donna Lutz
Morphology: John Alexander, Mike Minsky, Bruce Rosow
Text Selection: Sara Buckerfield, Jim Cloonan
Decodable Text: Jenny Hamilton, Steve Harmon

LANGUAGE! eReader is a customized version of the
CAST eReader for Windows® (3.0). CAST eReader
©1995—2003, CAST, Inc. and its licensors. All rights reserved.

University of Texas is a registered trademark of the University of Texas System. Harris Interactive is a registered trademark of Harris Interactive, Inc. Teenage Research Unlimited is a registered trademark of Teenage Research Unlimited, Inc. Cornell University is a registered trademark of the Cornell University Educational Corporation. Super Bowl is a registered trademark of the National Football League. NFL is a registered trademark of the National Football League. San Diego State University is a registered trademark of Aztec Shops Ltd.

ISBN 1-59318-320-8

Printed in the United States of America

Published and distributed by

SOPRIS
WEST
EDUCATIONAL SERVICES

4093 Specialty Place • Longmont, CO 80504 • (303) 651-2829
www.sopriswest.com

"It is possible to fly without motors but not without knowledge and skill."

—Wilbur Wright (1867–1912)

Table of Contents

This book contains six units.

Each unit builds knowledge in:

- Sounds and Letters
- Spelling and Words
- Vocabulary and Roots
- Grammar and Usage
- Listening and Reading
- Speaking and Writing

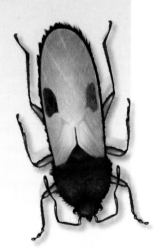

Unit 10   Take Time

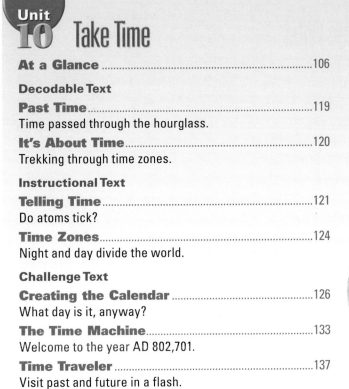

Unit 11 Catch the Wind

Appendix

Spin a Web

Unit 7 At a Glance

STEP 1

Phonemic Awareness and Phonics

Unit 7 has one consonant and one vowel sound: **x**, / ĕ /. Letters represent the sounds.

Consonants

Review: **x** represents two phonemes: / k / + / s / (tax / tăks /).

■ There is an alternate sound-spelling correspondence for the letter **x**.

x represents two other phonemes: / g / + / z / (exam / ĭg-zăm' /).

Vowels

■ The vowel is / ĕ / spelled **e** (bed / bĕd /).

Go to the **Vowel Chart** on page 204. Find ĕ for short / e / on the chart. Find the example word: **pet**.

The sound for the vowel is signaled by the use of a diacritical mark. The mark for short vowel sounds is the breve (˘): ă, ĕ, ĭ, ŏ, ŭ.

Word Recognition and Spelling

Using Unit 7 sound-spelling correspondences, we can read and spell words like these unit words: **bend, bet, egg, step, exam, exit.**

Spelling Tip: Adding -es

■ Nouns and verbs ending in **s**, **z**, or **x** add **-es** to form plural nouns or third person singular present tense verbs.

> **Plural Nouns**
>
> **dresses, fizzes, boxes**

> **Third Person Singular Present Tense**
>
> **presses, buzzes, waxes**

Contractions

■ **Contractions** are two words combined into one word. Some letters are left out and are replaced by an apostrophe ('). In Unit 7, the contractions are made with the word **not**.

> **Contraction With Not**
>
> **is + not = isn't**
>
> The letter **o** in **not** is replaced by the apostrophe (').

Unit 7 Contractions

aren't	weren't	didn't
isn't	doesn't	can't
wasn't	don't	

Unit 7 Essential Words

all	into	small
call	our	their

Spelling Lists

The Unit 7 spelling lists contain four word categories:

1. Words that use **e** to spell / ĕ / and **x** = / gz /

2. **Essential Words** (in italics)

3. Contractions with **not** spelled **n't**

4. Words with **-es** or **-ed** suffixes

Spelling Lists

Lessons 1–5		Lessons 6–10	
all	*our*	can't	invest
best	*small*	credit	jets
call	smell	didn't	pigpen
deck	test	dresses	rented
fell	*their*	exact	sled
into	web	exit	smelled
left	went	express	wasn't
nest		helped	

STEP 3

Vocabulary and Morphology

Unit Vocabulary

Sound-spelling correspondences from Unit 7 and previous units make up this unit's vocabulary.

■ What do these words mean?

■ Do some of them mean more than one thing? Which ones?

UNIT Vocabulary

e for / ĕ /

aspect	expect	left	press	tell
bed	express	leg	prospect	ten
bell	fell	less	red	tend
belt	felt	let	rent	tent
bend	get	men	rest	test
best	got	mend	sell	text
bet	held	mess	send	vest
bless	help	neck	sent	well
context	hen	nest	set	went
credit	index	net	sled	west
deck	insect	next	smell	yell
den	inspect	offset	speck	yes
dress	invest	passed	spell	yet
edit	jet	pen	spend	
egg	kept	pest	step	
end	led	pet	stress	

x = / gz /

exact	exam	exist	exit

Idioms

Review: Idioms are common phrases that cannot be understood by the meanings of their separate words—only by the entire phrase.

> **Idioms**
>
> be on your last leg = be unable to continue
>
> get off your back = have someone stop bothering you
>
> hit the deck = get out of bed

Expressions

■ **Expressions** are a common way of saying something. They occur often in English. They are similar to idioms. Expressions do not have a specific form. They are simply a common way of saying something.

> **Expressions**
>
> all wet = mistaken; on the wrong track
>
> in the wind = likely to happen
>
> odds and ends = mixed things; leftovers; pieces

Word Relationships: Homophones

■ Words that sound the same but have different meanings are called **homophones**. Examples: their/there; our/hour.

Word Relationships	What Is It?	Unit 7 Examples
antonyms	Words that have opposite meanings	best/worst; exit/ enter; get/give; yes/no
synonyms	Words that have the same or similar meaning	help/assist; exit/go; end/stop
attributes	Words that tell more about other words such as size, parts, color, and function	jets/fly; bell/rings; hen/clucks
homophones	Words that sound the same but have different meanings	their/there; our/hour

Meaning Parts

Review: Adding -**s** to most nouns makes them plural.
Example: jets

■ Adding -**es** to singular nouns ending in **s**, **z**, or **x** makes them plural.

> **Plural Nouns With -es**
>
> **dresses, fizzes, boxes**

Review: Adding endings to verbs signals number and tense (time).

-**s**	Signals third person singular, present tense. Example: bends
-**ing**	Adding -**ing** to verbs used with *am*, *is*, or *are* signals present progressive. Examples: am helping, is bending, are spelling

■ Adding -**ed** signals past tense. (See Step 4: Grammar and Usage.)

> **Past Tense**
>
> **jumped, swelled, tested**

■ The suffix -**ed** represents three sounds:

/ *t* / (jumped)

/ *d* / (swelled)

/ *ĭd* / (tested)

STEP

4

Grammar and Usage

Possessives

Review: **Pronouns** are function words used in place of nouns.
Nominative (subject) **pronouns** take the place of the subject in
a sentence. **Objective pronouns** take the place of objects in a
sentence.

■ Other pronouns show possession. They are called **possessive
pronouns**. **My, mine, your, yours, his, her, hers, its, our, ours,
their,** and **theirs** replace nouns or function as adjectives.

> **Possessives**
>
> **My** desk is a mess. (adjective)
>
> **Mine** is a mess. (pronoun)

Simple and Complete Subjects

Review: Nouns have several functions (or jobs). One function is
the subject of a sentence.

■ Nouns (or pronouns) serve as the **simple subject**
of a sentence.

> **Simple Subject**
>
> The blue **egg** fell from the nest.
>
> *Egg* is the simple subject.

■ The **complete subject** includes the noun (or pronoun) and all
of its modifiers.

> **Complete Subject**
>
> **The blue egg** fell from the nest.
>
> *The blue egg* is the complete subject.

Nouns can be subjects in sentences.

Unit 7 Nouns

bed	dress	hen	pen	swell
bell	egg	insect	pigpen	tent
belt	elk	jet	press	vet
bet	exit	leg	rent	west
credit	felt	lens	smell	
deck	glen	men	spell	
den	help	nest	stem	
desk	hem	net	step	

Compound Subjects

- A **compound subject** is two subjects joined by a conjunction.
- **Conjunctions** join words, phrases, or clauses in a sentence. Coordinating conjunctions are the most common type. They connect words with the same function. This unit focuses on the conjunction **and**.

> **Compound Subject**
>
> *Ellen* passed. Her *class* passed.
> *Ellen* + *class* = **compound subject** in the sentence:
> *Ellen* **and** *her class* passed.

The subjects *Ellen* and *class* are joined by the conjunction **and** to build a compound subject.

The diagram below shows the compound subject in this sentence.

Form: N + N/V   **noun + noun/verb**
Function: S + S/P   **subject + subject/predicate**

Ellen and her class passed.

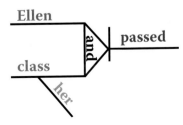

Past Tense Verbs: With -ed

- Verbs describe actions. Verbs also show time. If something happened yesterday, it is usually in the **past tense**.

- Add **-ed** to create regular past tense verb forms.

Tense Timeline

Yesterday	Today	Tomorrow
Past	Present	Future
-ed		

Unit 7 Verbs

Base Verb	Past Tense	Base Verb	Past Tense
deck	deck**ed**	mend	mend**ed**
end	end**ed**	pass	pass**ed**
exit	exit**ed**	rest	rest**ed**
help	help**ed**	smell	smell**ed**
inspect	inspect**ed**	spell	spell**ed**
invest	invest**ed**	test	test**ed**

STEP

5 Listening and Reading Comprehension

Informational and Narrative Text

- Some **informational** text is organized by **classification**. This text includes ideas, facts, evidence, or examples organized into categories. **Transition words** signal this organization.

> **Transition Words for Classification**
>
> the first kind, the second kind, the last kind
>
> one type, another type, a final type
>
> one reason, the next reason, another reason

- **Narrative** text tells a story. When we read a story, we listen or look for the parts of a story: characters, setting, events, and resolution.

Context Clues

- **Context clues** help us understand new vocabulary. Pronoun referents, meaning signals, and visuals, such as pictures, charts, and graphs, provide meaning links.

Signal Words

- Some sentences ask us to remember information from what we have read or heard. These sentences ask us to **Remember It**, or retrieve or recall information. They use specific signal words.

> **Signal Words for Remember It**
>
> recognize, state, list, locate, name

STEP 6

Speaking and Writing

We use different types of sentences when we speak and write.

Statements: Fact or Opinion

- Some sentences present facts or opinions. These are called **statements**.

> **Statements**
>
> **The Internet is called the Information Superhighway.**
> This tells us a fact about the Internet.
> What? It has another name, the Information Superhighway.
>
> **The World Wide Web has improved our future.**
> This expresses an opinion about the WWW.
> What? The WWW has improved our future.

Signal Words

- Some sentences ask for information. These sentences require retrieving information from memory to provide an answer. They use specific signal words.

> **Signal Words for Remember It**
>
> How do you **recognize** differences in e-mail addresses?
>
> **State** two types of articles found in newspapers.
>
> **List** three parts of e-mail addresses.
>
> **Locate** the items that may be found on a home page.
>
> **Name** the process to get photographs from the Web.

Paragraph Organization

- Some paragraphs are organized by **classification**, or categories. These paragraphs include ideas, facts, evidence, or examples organized by category. **Transition words** signal this organization. Examples: the first kind, the second kind, the last kind

More About Words

- **Bonus Words** use the same sound-spelling correspondences from Unit 7 and previous units.

- **Idioms** are common phrases that cannot be understood by the meanings of their separate words—only by the entire phrase.

- **Word History** tells the story of "ain't."

UNIT Bonus Words

annex	elk	legging	prep	tempt
asset	epic	lend	quest	tennis
beg	exotic	lens	sect	trend
bled	fed	lent	self	vent
blend	fleck	melt	sendoff	vet
bred	fled	met	septic	web
crept	flex	metric	sextet	wed
crest	glen	misled	skeptic	wept
dent	gremlin	peck	slept	wet
desk	hectic	peg	specs	yelp
desktop	hem	pelvic	sped	zest
dispel	instep	pelvis	spent	
ebb	intend	pent	stem	
eggnog	jell	pep	swell	
eggplant	jest	peptic	swept	

Idioms

Idiom	Meaning
be in the red	be operating at a loss; in debt
be on your last leg	be unable to continue
call it quits	stop working or trying
get down to brass tacks	begin talking about important things; get down to business
get off your back	have someone stop bothering you
get ripped off	be taken advantage of
get the ax	get fired
have a leg to stand on	have a good defense for your opinions or actions
hit the deck	get out of bed; fall or drop to a prone position; prepare for action
lend a hand	help someone

Why? Word History

Ain't—We aren't supposed to say it or write it. Where did it come from? *Ain't* has been around for centuries! The first form of *ain't* was "amn't" (a contraction for "am not"). People would say, "I'm helping, amn't I?" Then the pronunciation changed to *ain't*. Later, someone decided that *ain't* wasn't good English.

Today, we say, "I'm helping, aren't I?" We say "aren't I" because we have learned to avoid *ain't*. But we still hear it used informally for fun: "If it ain't broke, don't fix it!"

THE WORLD on the WEB

TEACHER: How much do you really know about the World Wide Web? The World Wide Web refers to all the Web sites in the world that people can visit using their computers! The Internet is a network of computers
5 that allows us to visit these sites. People are able to do various tasks while on "the Web." Read about the World Wide Web.

STUDENT: Kids log on to the World Wide Web. It is called "the Web." They log on with the Internet. It gives them
10 a path to the Web. They get text from the Web. Kids scan the text. Kids can jot down facts. They get film clips on the Web as well. The Web sends it all to their desktops. The Web spans the planet.

TEACHER: Some computers are also known as PCs. PC is
15 an abbreviation for "personal computer." The speed with which computers access information on the Web is incredible. Think about the days of going to the library and pulling books off the shelves to get information. Read about this ready access to
20 information.

STUDENT: Log on. Getting facts is quick. It is a snap. Step on an express track. The Web has facts on all topics. Kids use PCs. PCs help get the facts. Kids use them to draft their text. PCs let kids edit the facts. They print
25 the text. The job ends. Kids do their jobs fast on PCs.

TEACHER: Finding all the sites on the Web could be difficult without an address system. A series of letters

and numbers help us get to different sites. Read about the Web address system.

30 STUDENT: A Web site has an address. It has three parts. The first part can be www. This stands for "World Wide Web." It has a dot at the end. The next part gives a name. It has a dot at the end as well. The last part is a group. It does not have a dot at the end.

35 TEACHER: There are over 40 million Web sites in the world! You need a listing or directory to find the addresses for all of these sites. These listings can be found by using a Web browser or search engine. Learn more about what you can find when you use these
40 directories.

STUDENT: Look at an index on the Web. The list is endless. Get an address. Visit a class. Click. You can get a list of insects. The index has clinics. Click. You can get facts on jogging. "Dot coms" fill the list. Visit the NFL.
45 Click. You can get a list of mascots. Which site will you visit?

TEACHER: The World Wide Web has dramatically changed the speed with which we communicate and access information. Summarize the Web's impact.

50 STUDENT: Look at the past. The Web did not exist. We have it now. It gives facts in a snap. The Web spans the world. The Web sends it all to our desktops.

Log On!

TEACHER: Computers allow us to access the Internet and communicate instantly. It hasn't always been this way. Read about how much more efficient electronic mail, or e-mail, is compared to conventional mail.

5　**STUDENT:** In the past, mail was not fast. There were many steps. Step 1: Get a pen. Step 2: Get a pad of paper. Step 3: Draft text on the pad. Step 4: Get a stamp. Step 5: Drop the letter in the mailbox. The Web lets you skip steps. Sending mail can be quick. Get on the Web. A
10　computer lets you draft text. Next, click on "send." It is sent fast. Expect a prompt reply.

TEACHER: One of the most popular ways to use the Internet is for "chatting." People use e-mail and instant messaging (IM) to stay in touch. Read about chatting
15　on the Web.

STUDENT: Lots of kids log on. IM lets kids visit. Text is sent to pals. They send a fast reply. Kids chat online. There can be many replies. It can get hectic. Kids have a blast with IM.

TEACHER: A survey or poll is given periodically to young
people. It asks how they like to spend their free time.
The latest poll reveals a dramatic change in their
preferences. Read about the poll's results.

STUDENT: Kids spend lots of time on the Web. In the past,
25 the TV was on a lot. Now, it's on less. Kids are logged
on. This is a new trend. How can we tell? A survey was
drafted. It asked how kids spend their time. What topped
the list? Kids picked the Web. TV lost the top spot.

TEACHER: Adults need to pay attention to what children
30 view online. Read about how adults monitor children's
activities on the Web.

STUDENT: Adults have a job. Ads are sent on the Web.
Ads can tempt kids. Kids can be misled. They can be
tricked. Adults have to inspect the ads. They can block
35 the bad ads. They look at what is sent. They scan what
kids send back. They inspect the sites kids visit. Adults
can have a big impact.

World Wide Web

The Internet

Internet

a system connecting computers around the world

system

a group of related parts working together for a common purpose

We all use the **Internet**. Some use it every day. We're online. It connects us to the Web. We search for fun. We say we're surfing. We surf the Web. We use the Internet to search. What else do we call the

5 Internet? We also call it the *Information Superhighway*. It's true. The Internet is like a road **system**. It connects computers. It really is worldwide. What if you're in Hong Kong? What if you need information? It's in Mexico? The Internet gets it to you. Right now! We use the Web

10 every day. But how much do we know about it?

Web Speed

First, we know that we can find information on the Web fast. Do you use the Web for reports? Think about this. Before the Internet, where would you get information? You would have used many books.

15 You would have spent dozens of hours searching. That might not happen today. Today, if you need information, it's on the Web. It's at your fingertips. We can even get photographs. We can download them. Some come from the moon! We see them just as they're

20 sent to Earth. That's not just fast. It's immediate!

Web Address System

Second, the Web has its own address system.
The Web has millions of **links**. Finding one Web site
could become a cyberspace nightmare! But the Web
solves that problem. At home, your address might be
25 1111 Main Street. On the Web, you can have an address.
Your Web address could be: **roberto.en.utexas.edu**.
Who is Roberto? That's the person at the Web address.
The **.en** means English Department. The end, **.edu**,
stands for education. There are other endings. The
30 ending **.com** means **commercial**. The ending **.gov**
means government. The ending **.au** means Australia.
What about the address that begins with **utexas**? That
one is **unique**. It stands for University of Texas. Look
at your school's Web address. Can you explain how its
35 address identifies the school?

Web Organization

Also, the Web is organized in a special way. It is
made up of home pages. Home pages are usually the
first pages you see on a Web site. The pages contain
lots of things. They may be just words. They may have
40 pictures. Most home pages have both. Many have
video. A page might tell about a company. It might tell
about a school. It could tell about a person or a subject.
How do we **interact** with a home page? We choose a
link. We click on it. We get information! Most home
45 pages **link** to many other pages.

This first page on the NASA Web site is its home page.

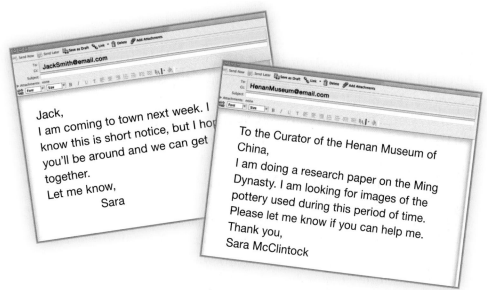

Jack,
I am coming to town next week. I
know this is short notice, but I hop
you'll be around and we can get
together.
Let me know,
    Sara

To the Curator of the Henan Museum of
China,
I am doing a research paper on the Ming
Dynasty. I am looking for images of the
pottery used during this period of time.
Please let me know if you can help me.
Thank you,
Sara McClintock

Web Conversations

Finally, the Web has e-mail. E-mail has changed
communication. Today, we connect in a new way. We
can talk to anybody, any place, any time. In seconds,
we contact someone. They can be across the planet.
50 It doesn't matter. E-mail saves us time. It helps us
work quickly. We can even keep records of our work
in special mailboxes. But e-mail is fun, too. It keeps
us in touch with friends. Do you think e-mail has
affected postal mail? Do you think it has affected
55 telephone calls? How do you see the future of Web
communication?

Answer It
Say each answer in a complete sentence.

1. State the meaning of WWW.
2. Name the process used to get photographs from
   the Internet.
3. How do you recognize the differences among the
   endings on Web addresses?
4. Locate the items that can be found on a home page.
5. How has e-mail changed communication?

Newspaper Connections

Newspaper Articles

Newspapers are full of articles about the local, regional, national, and international news of the day. Newspapers also contain many other kinds of articles. The two articles that follow are examples of articles you might find in your local newspaper. Neither is really news; however, they are types of articles that people read for information.

The first article, "Web of Lies," is an *opinion article.* It is a movie review. The writer gives an opinion about a new movie. Movie reviews are popular because they help people decide which movies they might like to see. But beware! The reviewer's opinion may not match your own.

The second article, "Web Wins!" is a *factual article.* It reports a new trend. It explains how something is changing. Factual articles usually contain data, or collections of numbers. Often, factual articles are based on polls. Polls are reports that tally the answers of the people who take part. This article, based on a poll, reports a trend in young people's recreation choices.

Web of Lies
Fictional movie review

MetroPress, June 6, 2002   Review by Emilio García

progresses
moves ahead; develops

LOS ANGELES—*Caught in a Web of Lies*. It was this summer's hottest movie! You've all heard about it.
5 It had six of Hollywood's hottest stars. One of them was Jenny Li. It had a multi-million dollar budget. *Web of Lies* was predicted to become
10 a top moneymaker. It was going to be a film classic. Last night, I went to see it.

The film opens with America's sweetheart in
15 tears (again). Jenny (yes, her character's name is also Jenny) is at the airport. She's leaving her friends in California. She's flying across the country to
20 the **Big Apple**. Jenny is in tears because she has to leave, but an old school friend needs her. Then just before she boards

the plane, something happens.
25 Jenny is on her cell phone. She's talking to somebody. And Jenny is scared.

As the story **progresses** (or doesn't), Jenny and her
30 friends are all caught up in the *Web of Lies* that surrounds Jenny. Someone doesn't like her. Some people are telling terrible lies about her. She
35 wants to know who it is, but she's afraid to find out. The plot thickens. In the end, guess what? Of course! Jenny comes out smelling like a rose.
40 Am I telling you to stay away from this film? No, of course not. You'll go anyway. The cast and the hype will pull you in. I'm just warning you.
45 It's a most **predictable** film. And at best, it's lukewarm.

Big Apple
a nickname for New York City

predictable
capable of being figured out ahead of time; expected

Answer It
Say each answer in a complete sentence.

1. List two types of articles found in newspapers.

2. Name the author of the movie review of *Caught in a Web of Lies*.

3. Where did Emilio García work?

4. Choose whether "Web of Lies" is a factual article or an opinion article. Explain your answer.

Web Wins!

In 2003, Harris Interactive and Teenage Research Unlimited found that young people spend an average of 16.7 hours a week *online* (not including e-mail), compared with 13.6 hours a week watching TV.

---

5 What do teenagers do for fun? For years, they watched TV. They spent more time with TV than any other activity. This is no longer true!
10 New figures are in. Today's teens spend more time on the Internet. They spend more time on the Web. They spend less time watching TV.
15 Reports show that time spent on the Web is going up. It is clear. Young people are using the Web. But until now, TV was tops. Today, the Web
20 wins. It is the most popular activity of young Americans. What is the source of this information? A Harris **poll** is the source. A total of 2,618
25 young people took the poll.

How was the poll taken? It was taken on the Web!

This poll **confirms** something parents and
30 teachers have known. Teens like to do more than one thing at a time. They watch TV. At the same time, they like sending instant messages.
35 They like getting e-mail. They like surfing the Web. How much time do they spend on the Web each week? They spend about 16.7 hours
40 on the Web. This does not include time writing and reading e-mail. How much time do they spend watching TV? They watch about 13.6
45 hours a week. What else do teenagers do? They listen to the radio for around 12 hours.

confirms
proves; shows to be true

poll
a way of counting different opinions

They talk on the phone for about 7.7 hours. Reading came in last. According to the poll, teenagers spend only six hours reading.

Teens today have grown up in a new way. Technology is a big part of their lives. They have computers. Computers are at school. Many young adults have computers at home, too. For today's teens, the Web has become a **permanent** part of life.

permanent
lasting forever

Answer It

Say each answer in a complete sentence.

1. What was the article about?

2. What happened?

3. Who polled the teenagers?

4. When did the poll take place?

5. Where did the teenagers report their answers for the poll?

6. What was the result of the poll?

Golden orb spiders.

The Strongest Web

In a dark corner, you may find one of nature's strongest materials. It's hard to see. You might miss it. When you brush into it, you'll know. Yes, you guessed it! It's a spider web! This web holds secrets to a
5 better world.

How did the web get there? Spiders spin fine silk thread. Then, they frame the web and hang it in midair. This is called "dragline silk." It is stronger than a steel wire of the same **diameter**. It is far more **elastic**. If
10 we had enough of this web's fiber, we could make better parachutes. We could make better artificial **ligaments**. We could even make better cables for suspension bridges.

Imagine a pencil. Then, imagine a rope of spider
15 silk the same diameter as the pencil. This silk might replace a three-centimeter-diameter steel cable. Where would we use it? We could use it on aircraft carriers. It could hook to the underside of airplanes. This would help airplanes land on ships' short runways. Randolph
20 Lewis, a scientist, says, "That's exactly what a spider's web is used for—to catch an object moving at full speed."

diameter
the width from one side of a circle to the other

elastic
capable of being stretched

ligaments
bands of strong tissue that connect bones or support other body parts

Making Webs

Can we create these strong webs? Can we make them elastic? Before we can, we have much to learn. Scientists are trying to figure out how spiders use ²⁵ **protein**. Their proteins are much like the proteins in our fingernails. At Cornell University, Lynn Jelinski studies golden spiders, or *Nephila clavipes*. They are large and easy to handle. They produce a strong dragline silk. To prevent fights among her spiders, ³⁰ each has its own cage in the lab. Lynn's research team collects and analyzes the silk from the spiders' webs. The team studies the silk's chemical composition and structure. They have found that the webs' silk polymer consists of three types of protein segments connected ³⁵ to each other. About one-third of the silk polymer is made of two types of crystals. The crystals give the silk its strength. Extremely **flexible** strands connect these crystals. These strands give the silk its elasticity. These two characteristics make silk that is strong and ⁴⁰ stretchable.

protein

a natural material found in all living things

flexible

easily bent without breaking

Research teams collect and analyze silk from spiders.

Spiders' webs cannot be obtained in large quantities like silkworm silk. But scientists are working on ways to **manufacture** it. One method is to implant spider silk genes into bacteria and yeast. This produces
45 proteins similar to those used by spiders. Then, scientists force the silk protein solution through a small opening to make silk. The resulting silk thread is not exactly like the silk of the spider's web, but it has similar properties.

manufacture

to make large quantities by hand or machine

Spin a Web!

50 Spiders make silk by combining protein molecules into long chains. Spiders have special glands. These glands produce proteins. Then, they force the proteins through a narrow duct to their spinnerets. When the proteins are in the duct, they start to combine. They
55 form a polymer. Now the spider is ready to spin a web. After the spider finishes its web, it often eats it! Why? Eating its web provides material for a new web!

Adapted from "Spinning Superstuff" by Steve Miller

Think About It

1. What is "dragline silk"?

2. List four ways that humans could use spiders' silk.

3. Compare the silk produced by spiders to the artificial spider silk produced by humans.

4. Describe how spiders make silk.

5. Why do you think it is important to prevent fights in the lab among golden spiders?

6. Think of three additional uses for spider silk that are not included in the article.

The Spider's Thread

A Folktale from Japan
by Akutagawa Ryunosuke.
Translated and adapted by Dean Durber.

fragrance

a sweet or pleasant smell or scent

Once upon a time, in a peaceful land, there was a beautiful lake full of floating white lilies. One fine morning, a man by the name of Shaka was taking a walk beside the lake, enjoying the sweet **fragrance** of
5 the flowers around him. He stood for a while admiring the beauty of the lake, when suddenly he saw a strange sight. Directly below the clear crystal waters he could see the mountains and rivers of another world, as if he were looking through a peephole. This was the land of
10 robbers and thieves.

Looking closely, he caught sight of Kandata, a man whom everybody knew had done many bad things. However, Shaka also remembered that once, many years ago, Kandata had spared the life of a little spider
15 he had seen in the woods. He had raised his foot to kill the spider, but had stopped and thought to himself, "How frightful! Although this spider is small, it is still a living creature. I will not kill it."

Because Shaka remembered Kandata's good deed,
20 he decided to try to help Kandata. **Fortunately**, by
the side of the lake there was a small spider sitting on a
jade-colored leaf weaving a thin thread. It so happened
that this was the same spider Kandata had saved that
day in the woods. The spider was only too happy to try
25 to repay the man who had spared his life. He willingly
gave Shaka some of his thread, which Shaka then took
in his hand and slowly fed down between the lilies to
the bottom of the lake.

Down in the world below, the robbers and thieves
30 spent their days bobbing up and down in muddy waters,
surrounded by dark, shadowy mountains. It was a lonely
place. The only sound that could be heard in the silence
was the breathing of the robbers themselves.

Kandata lifted his head out of the murky waters for
35 a moment, and managed to catch sight of the spider's
thin thread swaying in the darkness above. Quickly, he
stretched out his arms and grabbed it. "If I can just
get high enough to get out of this place, I can save
myself from sinking in the muddy waters below," he
40 said to himself.

He held on tightly to the thread and pulled himself
up with all his might. Higher and higher he went. For
years and years (for time here was very different from
time in the world above), he struggled to reach the top,
45 but there was a great distance between the two worlds.
No matter how far he climbed, it seemed as if he would
never reach the crystal waters of the land above.

Tired and weary, he could go no farther. Clinging
to the thread, he paused for a moment and looked
50 down into the distance far below him. He was
astonished to see just how far he had actually
climbed. The muddy waters and the **eerie** mountains
had long disappeared into the darkness below. Without
thinking, and somewhat foolishly, he gave out a loud
55 cry: "Hurray! Hurray! Look how far I have climbed!"

fortunately
luckily

jade
a green color

astonished
extremely surprised

eerie
mysterious and frightening

Just at that very moment, with his mouth still open, he remembered the other thieves and robbers down below. How stupid he had been! "What if they heard me and try to climb up using my thread?" he thought. He froze with fear. The thin thread could never carry the weight of all those people. If it broke, he would surely fall even deeper into the muddy waters than where he had come from.

Down below, the crowd of thieves had indeed heard his cry. They, too, started to make their way up the

spider's thread. On seeing this, Kandata wriggled and kicked and screamed out in terror. "Thieves, this is my thread! Who gave you **permission** to use it? Go back! Go back!"

70   There was the sudden sound of the thread snapping just above the point where Kandata was hanging. He could not be saved now. In an instant he fell, swirling like a spinning top into the darkness, down, down, down. Far above him, the spider's thread hung lifeless,

75 swaying in the starless sky.

    Watching all this from up above the clear waters, Shaka was sad at seeing how selfish Kandata had been. If only Kandata had not been so foolish, surely he could have saved himself, and maybe others, too.

80   The spider sitting on the jade-colored leaf continued to spin its thread. And Shaka continued on his walk. In the peaceful land above, it was almost noon.

permission
an approval; the right to

Think About It

1. As the folktale begins, who is walking along the lake?

2. What did Shaka see below the clear waters? Who lived there?

3. What does the story of the spider tell you about Kandata?

4. Describe Kandata's climb to the top. In what ways was his climb difficult?

5. How do you think Shaka felt about Kandata at the end of this folktale?

6. Folktales usually have some important meaning or some advice for the listener or reader. What do you think this folktale tells us about life?

Spider Woman

by Karen M. Leet

loom
a machine used to combine thread or yarn into cloth

weave
to cross threads over and under one another to make cloth

spindles
rods or pins on which fibers are spun

In Canyon de Chelly (pronounced kăn'yən də shā') in northeast Arizona, an ancient stone monument rises 832 feet from the canyon floor. The Navajo named it Spider Rock. According to Navajo legend, it was here
5 that Spider Man showed First Man how to build a **loom**. It is here where Spider Woman taught First Woman how to **weave** on the loom.

Spider Woman's four **spindles** were made of materials from all four directions of the Earth. North
10 was made of zigzag lightning and coal. South was made of flash lightning and turquoise. West was made of sheet lightning and abalone. East was made of a rain streamer and white shells. How beautiful her weaving must have been! Since that day, the Navajo have been
15 talented weavers. According to tradition, if a mother rubs a baby girl's tiny arm and hand with the web of a spider, the baby will grow into a skilled weaver. This poem tells of the beauty created by the mystic Spider Woman. It also thanks her for sharing the creative
20 craft of weaving.

> The Navajo call themselves Diné, meaning "The People." They were given the name Navajo by the Spanish and other Indians who lived nearby.

Spider Woman, Spider Woman, hear the people,
    hear the Diné calling you,
    hear the Diné speak your name.
Spider Woman in your **homeland**
25   deep beneath the world of sky,
    in your burrow, in your palace
    down below our world above,
    share your wisdom, share your goodness,
    share your skill at weaving beauty.
30 Weave the moonlight on the desert.
Weave the purple night beyond.
Weave the sweetly swaying treetops.
Weave the gently **lapping** water.
Weave the whispers of the wind.
35 Weave the hopes of all the people.
Weave in patterns of light and shadow.
Weave in colors deep and bright.
Weave in dreams of joy and **sorrow**.
Weave in time that lasts forever.

40 Spider Woman, Spider Woman, hear the people,
    hear the Diné calling you.
Weaver of silken web, the people
    thank you, for this gift of beauty,
    this gift of weaving you have given
45   and we give back to you.

homeland
one's place of birth

lapping
gently splashing or
slapping against

sorrow
a deep sadness

Think About It

1. Who are the Diné?

2. Where do you think Spider Woman lives? Why do you think so?

3. The Navajo believe that Spider Woman weaves beauty. Name six of the beautiful things she weaves.

4. Identify the line(s) of the poem that show that the Navajo are grateful to Spider Woman.

5. Is Spider Woman a woman? Is she a spider? Explain your answer.

6. Do the Navajo give a gift to Spider Woman? How do you know? Reread the poem's last line. Explain what you think it means.

Sing a Song

STEP 1

Phonemic Awareness and Phonics

Unit 8 introduces two types of consonant letter combinations.

Digraphs

■ **Digraphs** are two-letter graphemes that represent one sound.

ch	(chop, such)
sh	(ship, dish)
th	(thin, math) / *th* /
th	(this) / *th* /
wh	(when)
-**ng**	(sing)

Trigraphs

■ **Trigraphs** are three-letter graphemes that represent one sound. In Unit 8, the trigraph is:

-**tch**   (match)

Go to the Consonant Chart on page 203. Find the sounds for these letters: **ch**, **sh**, **th** (thin), **th** (this), **wh**, -**ng**.

STEP 2

Word Recognition and Spelling

Using Unit 8 consonant letter combinations, we can read and spell words like these unit words: **chill**, **fish**, **moth**, **this**, **when**, **sing**, **patch**, **sink.**

Spelling Tip: ch- or -tch

■ The sound / *ch* / is represented two ways. The position of / *ch* / in a word helps you spell it:

1. Use **ch** at the beginnings of words.

> **ch-**
> **ch**at, **ch**ip, **ch**op, **ch**ess

2. Use **-tch** after a short vowel at the ends of one-syllable words.

> **-tch**
> ma**tch**, pi**tch**, bo**tch**, fe**tch**

Exceptions include: much, such, rich, and which.

Saying -nk

■ The letters **-nk** represent two separate sounds: / *ng* / and / *k* /. The letter combination **-nk** is not a digraph.

> **-nk**
> ba**nk**, pi**nk**, thi**nk**

Notice the differences in these sounds: / *n* /, / *ng* /, / *nk* /.

ban	bang	bank
pin	ping	pink
thin	thing	think

Compound Words

Review: **Compound words** are words made up of two or more smaller words. In a compound word, the smaller words are real words that can stand alone. Example: cat + fish = catfish

Unit 8 Compound Words

anything	chopsticks	whiplash
anywhere	eggshell	within
backlash	flashback	without
backstretch	offspring	
catfish	shellfish	

Spelling Tip: Adding -es

Review: Add **-es** to nouns and verbs ending in **s**, **z**, or **x** to form plural nouns (faxes), or third person singular present tense verbs (flexes).

■ This is also true for nouns and verbs ending in **ch**, **sh**, or -**tch**.

> **Plural Nouns With -es**
> rich**es**, dish**es**, match**es**

> **Third Person Singular Present Tense Verbs With -es**
> pinch**es**, wish**es**, patch**es**

Unit 8 Essential Words

about	many	word
any	out	write

Spelling Lists

The Unit 8 spelling lists contain four word categories:

1. Words with the consonant digraphs and trigraph: <u>ch</u>, <u>sh</u>, <u>th</u>, <u>wh</u>, -<u>ng</u>, -<u>tch</u>
2. **Essential Words** (in italics)
3. Compound Words
4. Words with -**s**, -**es**, -**ed**, or -**ing** suffixes

Spelling Lists

Lessons 1–5		Lessons 6–10	
about	song	anything	long
any	thank	bath	patches
bank	think	benches	pitched
chick	when	cashed	shop
many	wish	catch	sink
math	*word*	chipped	thin
out	*write*	fishing	without
ship		kings	

Vocabulary and Morphology

Unit Vocabulary

Sound-spelling correspondences from this Unit 8 and previous units make up this unit's vocabulary.

- What do these words mean?

- Do some of them mean more than one thing? Which ones?

UNIT Vocabulary

ch, sh, th, wh, -ng, -tch

bank	drink	pink	than
bath	ethic	pitch	thank
bench	ethnic	ranch	that
blank	fish	rang	them
blink	flash	rich	then
branch	gang	ring	thick
bring	hang	scratch	thin
catch	hitch	shall	thing
check	honk	shift	think
chest	inch	ship	this
chick	ink	shop	when
chill	king	sing	which
chin	link	sink	whip
chip	long	song	wing
chop	mash	spring	wink
cloth	match	sting	wish
crank	mink	stink	with
crash	moth	string	within
dash	patch	strong	
dish	path	swing	

Word Relationships

Word Relationships	What Is It?	Unit 8 Examples
antonyms	Words that have opposite meanings	thin/thick; catch/toss; sink/float; in/out
synonyms	Words that have the same or similar meaning	patch/fix; pitch/toss; scratch/itch
homophones	Words that sound the same but have different meanings	write/right
attributes	Words that tell more about other words, such as size, parts, color, or function	fish/swim; moth/flies; chicks/scratch

Meaning Parts

Review: Adding **-s** to most nouns makes them plural. Example: moths

- Adding **-es** to singular nouns ending in **s**, **z**, or **x** makes the nouns plural. This is also true for nouns ending in **ch**, **sh**, or **tch**.

> **Plural Nouns With -es**
> **riches, dishes, matches**

Review: Adding **-s** signals third person singular, present tense for most verbs. Example: shops

- Adding **-es** also signals third person singular, present tense verbs.

> **Third Person Singular Present Tense Verbs With -es**
> **branches, wishes, pitches**

Review: Adding **-ing** to verbs used with *am*, *is*, or *are* signals present progressive. Examples: am singing, is pitching, are shopping

Review: Adding **-ed** signals past tense. Examples: chipped, chilled, botched

Grammar and Usage

Regular and Irregular Past Tense Verbs

Review: Verbs describe actions. Verbs also show time. If something happened yesterday, it is usually in the **past tense**.

Review: Add **-ed** to create regular past tense verb forms.

Tense Timeline

Yesterday	Today	Tomorrow
Past	Present	Future
-ed		

Unit 8 Verbs (Regular)			
Base Verb	**Regular Past Tense**	**Base Verb**	**Regular Past Tense**
blink	blink**ed**	fish	fish**ed**
cash	cash**ed**	match	match**ed**
chat	chatt**ed**	patch	patch**ed**
check	check**ed**	scratch	scratch**ed**
chip	chipp**ed**	shift	shift**ed**
chop	chopp**ed**	shop	shopp**ed**
crash	crash**ed**	wish	wish**ed**

- Some verbs signal time through irregular verb forms. These verbs from Units 1–7 and Unit 8 below have irregular past tense forms.

Verbs (Irregular)

Base Verb	Irregular Past Tense	Base Verb	Irregular Past Tense
be	was/were	say	said
do	did	sell	sold
fit	fit	send	sent
get	got	sit	sat
give	gave	stand	stood
have	had	stick	stuck
hit	hit	swim	swam
let	let	win	won

Unit 8 Verbs (Irregular)

Base Verb	Irregular Past Tense	Base Verb	Irregular Past Tense
bring	brought	spring	sprang
catch	caught	string	strung
drink	drank	swing	swung
ring	rang	think	thought
sing	sang	write	wrote

Simple and Complete Predicates

Review: The predicate part of the sentence contains the main verb of the sentence.

- Verbs serve as the **simple predicate** of a sentence.

> **Simple Predicate**
>
> The class **clapped** during the song.
>
> *Clapped* is the simple predicate.

- The **complete predicate** includes the verb and all of its modifiers.

> **Complete Predicate**
>
> The class **clapped during the song**.
>
> *Clapped during the song* is the complete predicate.

Compound Predicates

- A **compound predicate** is two verbs joined by a conjunction.

> **Compound Predicate**
>
> The class *sang.*
>
> The class *clapped.*
>
> The class *sang* **and** *clapped.*

The verbs *sang* and *clapped* are joined by the conjunction **and** to build a compound predicate.

The diagram below shows the compound predicate in this sentence.

Form: N/V + V   **noun/verb + verb**
Function: S/P + P   **subject/predicate + predicate**

The class sang and clapped.

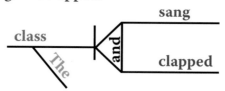

Listening and Reading Comprehension

Informational and Narrative Text

- Some **informational** text is organized by **classification**. This text includes ideas, facts, evidence, or examples organized into categories. **Transition words** signal this organization.

> **Transition Words for Classification**
>
> the first kind, the second kind, the last kind
>
> one type, another type, a final type
>
> one reason, the next reason, another reason

- **Narrative** text tells a story. When we read a story, we listen or look for the parts of a story: characters, setting, events, and resolution.

Context Clues

- **Context clues** help us understand new vocabulary. Pronoun referents, meaning signals, and visuals, such as pictures, charts, and graphs, provide meaning links.

Signal Words

- Some sentences ask us to remember information from what we have read or heard. These sentences ask us to **Remember It**, or recall or retrieve information. They use specific **signal words**.

> **Signal Words for Remember It**
>
> recall, retrieve, repeat, describe

6

Speaking and Writing

We use different types of sentences when we speak and write.

Statements: Fact or Opinion

■ Some sentences present facts or opinions. These are called **statements**.

> **Statements**
>
> **Woody Guthrie wrote "This Land Is Your Land."**
> This tells us a fact about Woody Guthrie.
> What? He wrote the song "This Land Is Your Land."
>
> **Woody Guthrie is America's favorite songwriter.**
> This expresses an opinion about Woody Guthrie as a songwriter.
> What? He is America's favorite songwriter.

Signal Words

■ Some sentences ask for information. These sentences require retrieving information from memory to provide an answer. They use specific **signal words**.

> **Signal Words for Remember It**
>
> **Recall** when whales sing.
>
> **Retrieve** the name of Woody Guthrie's greatest song.
>
> **Repeat** the elements of a whale song.
>
> **Describe** the purpose of a whale song.

Paragraph Organization

■ Some paragraphs are organized by **classification**, or categories. These paragraphs include ideas, facts, evidence, or examples organized by category. **Transition words** signal this organization. Examples: one type, another type, a final type

More About Words

■ **Bonus Words** use the same sound-spelling correspondences we have studied in this unit and previous units.

■ **Idioms** are common phrases that cannot be understood by the meanings of their separate words—only by the entire phrase.

■ **Word History** explains the origin of the digraph **th**.

UNIT Bonus Words

anything	fifth	sang	spank
anywhere	filth	sank	sprang
ash	flesh	sapling	stench
bang	fling	sash	stitch
batch	frank	shack	strength
blacksmith	gash	shaft	swish
brink	gong	shed	switch
broth	hatch	shellfish	tank
cash	itch	shin	tenth
catfish	lash	shock	theft
chant	latch	shot	thickness
chap	length	shrank	thrift
chat	math	shrill	thrill
chess	mesh	shrimp	throng
chimp	notch	shrink	trash
clang	pinch	sketch	trench
clash	plank	slang	twitch
cling	polish	slash	whim
depth	quench	sling	witch
ditch	rank	smash	yank
drank	rash	smith	
fetch	rink	snatch	

Idioms	
Idiom	**Meaning**
be on the blink	be out of working order
be within an inch of	be almost to the point of
catch you in the act	catch you doing something illegal or private
get it off your chest	let go of your pent-up feelings
give it your best shot	try as hard as you can to accomplish something
have you in stitches	have you laughing uncontrollably
ring a bell	arouse an indistinct memory
sink or swim	fail or succeed on your own
stick your neck out	take a risk
wing it	go through a situation or process without any plan

Word History

Digraph th—Anglo-Saxon scribes (writers) created some letters the Roman alphabet did not have. Two of these letters were named *Thorn* (þ) and *Eth* (ð). *Thorn* and *Eth* represented two Anglo-Saxon sounds (phonemes). These sounds did not exist in Latin. The Roman alphabet had no letters to represent these sounds. Anglo-Saxon scribes created new symbols to represent these sounds: / *th* / (as in *thin*); and / *th* / (as in *this*).

Today, Modern English represents both of the sounds with the same pair of letters: **th**.

Singing Whales

TEACHER: Imagine yourself on a whale-watching trip. What you will hear is just as amazing as what you will see.

STUDENT: A ship is moving off the dock. Quick, get on. It
5 is tracking whales. Not to catch them. To catch their songs! Whales sing. It's a fact. Their singing is fantastic! They live in the depths, yet their songs get to the top. They can sing at length. A song can last 10 hours! Whales can sing many pitches. The pitch in the song
10 can be shrill. The pitch can be soft. It can blast. Whales can trill in a song. Pitches link and make a song.

TEACHER: How much do you know about whales?

STUDENT: The whale is the biggest living mammal. It swims past the ship. Inspect it. Its skin is black. It has
15 a gloss to it. It can have a fin on its back. This is not an exotic fish. In fact, it is not a fish at all! It is a mammal. Fish have gills. Whales have lungs. There are two classes of whales. The first class has teeth. The second class does not. The first class tracks fish
20 and squid to eat. The second class gets the smallest fish.

They eat small shrimp and plants as well. They trap them as they drink. The living things are sifted in the whale's mouth.

TEACHER: We know many creatures live in groups. Ants
25 live in colonies. Geese live in a flock. Guess what you call a group of whales?

STUDENT: Whales can live in a gam. This is called a pod as well. This is a small group of about 20. They swim as a gam. They sing as a gam. This kinship can help them
30 live. It helps fend off whales that kill.

TEACHER: What are the songs like?

STUDENT: In a gam, the whales sing a song. All the pitches match. They are calling with songs. The songs tell things. When you spot a whale, sing with him. Get your
35 song to match his! This song can help you relax.

A Man and His Songs

TEACHER: Woody Guthrie is considered to be the father of American folk music. His early years were filled with both happiness and hardship. Read about his life when he was young.

5   STUDENT: Woody lived from 1912 to 1967. He lived with sadness. There were many setbacks. His dad lost many jobs. His family lived where his dad had jobs. They had cash now and then. His mom offset the sadness. His mom sang to Woody. His granddad helped. His
10 granddad sang as well. His family helped Woody sing. Songs helped him express himself. His dad left when Woody was 11. His dad went west. Woody missed his dad. He lived with his mom. Then, his mom got sick. She left. She had to live in a clinic.

15 TEACHER: At 13, Woody was alone. He went to live with a foster family but soon set out to travel and earn a living. He began working a series of odd jobs. These experiences would influence his songs.

STUDENT: Woody drifted from job to job. He drilled wells.
20 He picked crops. At 16, he got a guitar as a gift. He did odd jobs. He sang for a living. His songs backtracked to his past. The songs were from his mom and granddad. From them, he crafted a new sound. The past lived on in his songs. His songs were linked with his past. He
25 had to live. For his living, he did many things. His jobs led him across the land.

TEACHER: As Woody traveled across America, he was inspired by its natural beauty. This theme resounds through his music.

30 **STUDENT:** Woody's treks prompted his songs. This vast land impressed him. He was thinking of the grand hills. He was thinking of the land's riches. He wrote "This Land Is Your Land." The song expressed his thinking. It was a big hit then. It is still a hit. He wrote many 35 songs. His songs have had an impact.

TEACHER: He overcame many hardships and much sadness as a young man. As Woody grew older, he had to face more sorrow and pain. He became very ill. Read about these years.

40 **STUDENT:** Woody kept writing songs. Then, he got sick. His illness left him helpless. It was sad. Woody is missed. His songs live on. Songs are his lasting gift. We still sing them.

WHALE Song

An Old Song

Sailors have listened to whale song for thousands of years. It fascinates us. Roger Payne studies it. He asks a question. What are these songs? We did not know. Now, we are beginning to understand. The songs are

5 messages. But what do they mean?

Parts of the Song

A whale's song has many parts. First, there is an *element*. An element is one sound. Elements can be long groans. They can be low moans. They can be roars. They can be trills. They can be cries. They can

10 be snores. They can be growls, whistles, or chirps. Another part of a whale's song is a *phrase*. Elements repeat in patterns. Two to four different elements repeat. This makes a short sound string. We call the strings *phrases*. The last part of a whale's song is the

15 *theme*. Whales repeat phrases several times. A set of similar phrases is a *theme*. Whales sing from one theme to the next. They do not **pause**.

pause
to stop for a moment

Whale songs are very long. A song may have seven
or eight themes. They sing themes in an order, from
20 first to last. One song lasts 10 to 30 minutes. The songs
prove whales have amazing memories. When a song
ends, whales **surface** to breathe. Then, they begin to
sing again. They start over from the first theme.

surface
to rise to the top

Time for Singing

Whales sing when they migrate. Whales migrate
25 in the fall. They leave the northern waters. They swim
to the tropics. They sing while they swim to warmer
waters. They sing again during their migration back
north. Whales often don't sing in early spring or late
summer.

Who Sings?

30 Not all whales sing. Only males make whale songs.
A singing male swims alone. He stays underwater for
a long time. He stays in a small area. He comes up to
breathe. He does this every 8 to 15 minutes.

Purposes of Whale Song

Whales sing for many reasons. First of all, the
35 songs are not just for entertainment. The songs set
guidelines for the group. They communicate with
the group. The role of whale song is similar to that of

guidelines
rules

"Some of my happiest hours have been spent at night
lying back in the cockpit of a sailboat, alone on watch,
steering with one foot and watching the mast sweeping
across vast fields of stars, while the songs of the
humpback whales poured up out of the sea, to fill my
head, my heart and finally my soul as well."

—Roger Payne, whale researcher

Humpback whales in the singing position.

bird song. It guides behavior. It can stop competition. Without the songs, what would happen? Groups would
40 split during migration. Feeding and behavior would not be **coordinated** . In addition, a whale song can advertise. It invites mates. Whale songs attract females.

coordinated
organized to work well together

Singing a New Song

There is an interesting fact about the songs of whales. They change. Each year's song is a little
45 different. The whales make changes during the singing season. The season goes along. Then, all together, the whales change their songs. The changes are small. They may change just two or three sounds. The **basic** patterns stay the same. For example, moans may
50 change from long to short. But they are still moans.

basic
original; necessary

We don't know why they change their song. Maybe a dominant male decides on the song. Maybe he controls the song for a year. It may be that the new song interests the females. Whatever the reason, the 55 whales in the area sing this new song.

Whale songs fascinate us. At last, we are learning how they communicate. One day, we may connect with them. When we do, it will probably be with song.

Adapted in part from "Whale Song" from "Oceans Alive: Whale Dreams" by permission of the Australian Broadcasting Corporation. ABC Online: www.abc.net.au/oceans/whale/song.htm.

"As you sit in your boat, lightly borne on the night sea, watching the weather and the stars and the sails, it all seems so simple, regular, ordinary, and you have no thought of how far beneath you the **abyss** extends. But then you put on headphones, and after a while a whale starts to sing, and the echoes from the abyss come tumbling and roaring back, and suddenly you are aware of the vastness of the mystery that underlies your boat."

—Roger Payne, whale researcher

abyss
a huge, bottomless space

Answer It
Say each answer in a complete sentence.

1. Repeat the parts of a whale song.

2. Retrieve information that tells when whales sing.

3. Recall the gender of the whale that sings.

4. Describe the purposes of whale song.

5. How do you recognize if a whale has changed its song?

Woody's Song

This land is your land;
this land is my land
From California,
to the New York island.
From the redwood forest,
to the Gulf Stream waters,
This land was made
for you and me.

—Woody Guthrie,
America's songwriter

symbol

a thing that stands
for something
very important or
meaningful

**Great
Depression**

a long period of
economic slow-
down and unem-
ployment during
the 1930s

How many times have you sung "This Land Is Your
Land"? Many think this song is one of the best. It is
about the American people. It was written by Woody
Guthrie. Woody himself is an American **symbol**. He
5 was a singer and songwriter. Woodrow Wilson Guthrie
was born in 1912. He was born in a small town in
Oklahoma.

At 16, Woody discovered the guitar. It was like
magic! He began spinning musical tales. Woody told
10 musical stories of the **Great Depression**. He spun

songs about Oklahoma's hard **Dust Bowl** days. He sang simple songs. He sang complex songs. Sometimes, he sang silly songs for kids. Woody was a wanderer. When he was 28 years old, he found his way to New

15 York City. Here, he settled down. He raised a family. He was singing and playing all the way.

In 1952, Woody was told he had a terrible illness. He was 40 years old. The illness was called Huntington's. Woody became weaker and weaker. His body

20 degenerated. Bravely, he carried on. Woody continued writing songs. He died 15 years later. It was 1967.

Woody's daughter, Nora, has many fond memories of her father and his music. "Music—the guitar, the fiddle, the **mandolin**—was as much a part of our

25 household as the couch, the bed, or the chair," she explained. "We really lived with all the music, all this art. It wasn't like they were something **precious** on the shelf, something you never touched. You know, he'd write a song and it would sit on our table. You might

30 have chocolate milk, and it might spill, and there might be these little stains." Not to worry, though, she said. "He'd just write another one. A little chocolate milk stain

35 didn't matter."

Woody loved children. "He was very childlike himself," Nora said. "His guitar and his children's songs were his way of

40 talking to us. Instead of saying, 'Now kids, I told you to clean up your room,' he would sing, 'Clean-oh, clean-oh, clean.' Instead of saying, 'Don't hit

45 each other,' like another father would, he'd sing 'Don't you

Dust Bowl
the period of powerful dust storms that destroyed crops in the midwestern and southern plains in the 1930s

mandolin
a high-pitched, stringed musical instrument

precious
extremely valuable; costly

push me, push me, push me down.' Whatever teachings he gave us were in his music."

Woody's talent was music. He also was a talented
50 artist. Nora remembers many art projects she did with Woody and her brother, Arlo. Today, Nora is **preserving** her father's music and art. Woody's autobiography, *Bound for Glory*, is full of his wonderful drawings. Nora also has worked on a picture book for
55 children. The book is called *This Land Is Your Land*.

Woody's songs were gifts to all of us. But Woody's greatest song was "This Land Is Your Land." It's not a song just about our country. It is a song about the beauty of our land and our world. It is a song for all
60 people, everywhere. When you're feeling a little down, sing Woody's song.

preserving

maintaining; keeping in good condition

Adapted from "Woody's Music" by Barbara Hall

Nora, Woody's daughter, is preserving her father's music and art.

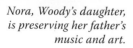

Answer It
Say each answer in a complete sentence.

1. Who was Woody Guthrie?

2. What did he do?

3. When was Woody born? When did he die?

4. Where did Woody grow up? Where did he raise his family?

5. What did Nora's descriptions tell about Woody as a father?

HMONG SONG

During the Vietnam War and its aftermath, thousands of Hmong (pronounced mawng) people were forced from their homes. They fled Laos and Thailand. Many came to America in search of a better life. When
5 they arrived in their new country, they brought with them a **wealth** of musical tradition.

Hmong song is an **integral** part of Hmong culture. It is used in rituals like those of courtship and death.

Hmong Language

To understand Hmong song, it is important to
10 know something about the Hmong language. Like many Asian languages, the Hmong language is tonal. A word's meaning depends on more than **pronunciation** . It also depends on its tone, or pitch. In addition, word meaning depends on whether the voice rises or falls. In a way,
15 Hmong language *is* song.

From Language to Song

Hmong language **intertwines** with Hmong music. Hmong songs themselves are a kind of language. Hmong musicians can play an entire song lyric— without ever singing a word! Hmong poetry is always
20 sung. One Hmong instrument, the *qeej* (pronounced kĕng), is highly regarded. It is made from six bamboo

wealth
a large amount

integral
essential; necessary

pronunciation
the way of saying a word

intertwines
combines, mixing parts of each

pipes attached to a wooden wind chamber. The qeej is linked to Hmong language. Four of its six pipes represent the tones spoken by the Hmong.

The Song of the Leaf

25 Hmong instruments may be simple or complex. The qeej is very complex. But the Hmong also play a much simpler instrument. It is the leaf. It is as important to Hmong song as the qeej. What kind of leaf can be an instrument? Just about any leaf taken 30 from a tree can be played. But this is not easy. Leaf songs are **intricate** and difficult to learn.

In the hills of Laos and in Thailand, leaf blowing was used for hundreds of years. The sound traveled far. People sent messages across distant mountains. It 35 was almost like using a telephone. To communicate, a person had to learn the leaf-blowing language. Different tunes had different meanings. It was not so hard to hear the meaning. Learning how to play the leaf took lots of practice.

intricate

having many parts or details

From Qeej to Break Dancing

40 The Hmong brought new traditions to America. Once here, they began to add American styles to their traditions. For example, many Hmong Americans are very good at break dancing. Why are they so good at it? The song of their culture gives them a definite edge.

"Momentum" triptych oil on canvas, by Vietnamese American artist Nhon Nguyen.

Many Hmong Americans are good at break dancing. What makes them so good at it?

45 The qeej is always played while dancing. When Hmong
students learn to play the qeej, they also learn specific,
intricate dance steps. The dance is difficult and is an
important cultural tradition. Today's qeej players have
expanded the tradition. When they play qeej **solos**,
50 these talented dancers expand the traditional qeej
dance steps with break-dancing moves.

solos

performances done
by one person alone

*These young girls are performing a
traditional Hmong dance.*

Think About It

1. What are the ancestral countries of the Hmong people?

2. What is unique about the Hmong language?

3. Describe a similarity between the instrument called the *qeej* (kĕng) and the Hmong language.

4. In their homeland, the Hmong used leaf-blowing to communicate. List the devices you use to send messages. How are these devices different from the technique of leaf-blowing?

5. Hmong performers have blended traditional qeej music with American break-dancing moves. Name some of your ancestors' cultural traditions.

6. Some say there are two ways immigrants can fit into American culture. One way is the "melting pot." In this way, immigrants shed their cultural identities and blend into society. The other way is the "salad bowl." Immigrants hold on to their unique ethnic traditions when they join American society. Discuss the advantages and disadvantages of each way.

The POWER of Song

Just about everyone agrees that song can be inspiring. It also can be depressing. It can be entertaining or energizing. Can song also be empowering? That question was answered one
5 beautiful afternoon in Edinburgh, Scotland, in 1990, during the British **equivalent** of the American Super Bowl. The answer was "yes."

The Corries

Ronnie Browne and Roy Williamson, known as the Corries, were Scotland's most popular folk duo. In
10 the 1970s, they recorded a song that became a symbol for their country and its people. The song, "The Flower of Scotland," was written by Roy Williamson. It was about Scotland's past and its future. When the Corries recorded "The Flower of Scotland," it
15 became an instant hit. The song is now included on their records and in all their performances. Over the years, the song has become a symbol of Scotland's hopes for independence. It is now known as Scotland's **unofficial** national anthem.

The Game

20 In 1990, the Scottish rugby (football) team hosted the English team at Murray Field in Edinburgh. It was the final match of the Five Nations Championship.

equivalent
something that is equal to another

unofficial
not valid or certified

The final match has the same importance in Britain as the Super Bowl has in the United
25 States. In this match, the English team was the unchallenged favorite. Scotland had won its place in the final. But they had won almost by accident. Scotland was no match for the powerful English team.

The Song

30 Both teams lined up. The crowd stood as the national anthem was played. The teams were ready for the kickoff. But before they could start the game, a **pipe band** walked onto the field! The band began to play "The Flower of Scotland." Immediately, the 50,000
35 Scots in the stadium joined in, singing:

> *Flower of Scotland, when will we see your like again?*
> *That fought and died for your wee bit o' hill and glen*
> *And stood against him, Proud Edward's army*
> *And sent him homeward, to think again.*[1]

pipe band
a group playing bagpipes

spectators
people watching an event

emotion
a strong feeling

dominated
controlled; held power over

The People

40 There wasn't a dry Scottish eye in the place. And it wasn't only the **spectators** who were moved. The commentators covering the match for BBC television and radio became silent. They couldn't speak because of the **emotion** of the moment. Even
45 the proud English felt the tension in the air. The band's playing and the Scots' singing had created an energy.

The Energy

It was like a fairy tale. The Scots **dominated** the game from the start.
50 Despite all predictions that they would lose, they outplayed the English team.

[1] Refers to the defeat of King Edward II's English army by King Robert the Bruce's Scottish army at Bannockburn in 1314. ©The Corries Music Ltd.

The Scots won. Imagine a Super Bowl. Imagine the best NFL team being beaten by the worst. That was just what happened in 1990 in the final match of the
55 Five Nations Championship.

The Power of Song

After the game, all the Scottish players agreed. They said that the pipes and the singing from the stands had given them the edge they needed. The song had done it. It was what they needed to beat the much
60 better English team. That is power—the power of song.

Adapted from "The Power of Song" by Bob Black

Think About It

1. The first paragraph says that a song can be inspiring, depressing, entertaining, energizing, or empowering. Do you agree? Why or why not?

2. Who were the Corries?

3. Name the title of the song that had power.

4. Where did the game take place?

5. The author said that "Even the proud English felt the tension in the air." Explain what you think the author meant. What had created the tension? How do you think this tension affected how the English played?

6. What do you think the author meant by the title "The Power of Song"?

Bug Us

STEP 1

Phonemic Awareness and Phonics

Unit 9 has two vowel sounds: / ŭ / and / o͝o /.

Vowels

- The letter **u** represents two different vowel sounds:

  / ŭ / (sun)

  / o͝o / as in book (put)

- The letter **o** also represents / ŭ / (from).

Go to the **Vowel Chart** on page 204. Find ŭ on the chart. Find the example word: **cup**. Find o͝o on the chart. Find the example word: **put**.

The sound for the vowel is signaled by the use of a diacritical mark. The mark for short vowel sounds is the breve (˘): ă, ě, ĭ, ŏ, ŭ.

STEP 2

Word Recognition and Spelling

Using Unit 9 sound-spelling correspondences, we can read and spell words like these unit words: **bug, trust, much, push, pull**.

Spelling Tip: / ŭ / Spelled o

Some words keep an Old English spelling for the / ŭ / sound. In these words, the vowel sound is spelled with the letter **o**.

> **/ ŭ / Spelled o**
>   **front, shove, ton**

Compound Words

Review: **Compound words** are words made up of two or more smaller words. In a compound word, the smaller words are real words that can stand alone. Example: bath + tub = bathtub

Unit 9 Compound Words		
backup	drumstick	humpback
bulldog	dustpan	manhunt
checkup	fullback	nutshell
chestnut	gumdrop	stinkbug
cutback	handcuff	sunlamp

Syllables

Review: All words have at least one syllable. A syllable is a word part that has one vowel sound. The number of vowel sounds equals the number of syllables in a word. Many words have more than one syllable. The words below have two syllables. Note the pattern of vowels (V) and consonants (C):

$$\textbf{pub} + \textbf{lic} = \textbf{public}$$
$$\text{vc} + \text{cv} = \text{vc/cv}$$

These Unit 9 two-syllable words have the VC/CV pattern.

VC/CV			
chipmunk	muffin	rustic	suffix
instruct	public	submit	summit
insult	publish	subset	until

Contractions

Review: **Contractions** are two words compressed into one word. Some letters are left out and are replaced by an apostrophe (').
In Unit 9, the contractions are made with the word **would**.

> **Contraction With Would**
>
> I + **would** = **I'd**
> The letters **woul** in **would** are replaced with an apostrophe (').

Unit 9 Contractions	
I'd	we'd
you'd	you'd
he'd, she'd, it'd	they'd

Unit 9 Essential Words

been	should	two
could	too	would

Spelling Lists

The Unit 9 spelling lists contain four word categories:

1. Words with / ŭ / spelled **u** or **o** and words with / o͝o / spelled **u**
2. **Essential Words** (in italics)
3. Compound Words
4. Words with **-s** or **-es**, **-ed**, or **-ing** suffixes

Spelling Lists

Lessons 1–5		Lessons 6–10	
been	scrub	bushes	pulling
bug	*should*	chipmunk	rubbed
could	shove	clubs	running
cut	thrust	dusted	she'd
done	*too*	income	something
front	*two*	instruct	sunlit
push	*would*	much	they'd
rush		nutmeg	

Vocabulary and Morphology

Unit Vocabulary

Sound-spelling correspondences from Unit 9 and previous units make up this unit's vocabulary.

- What do these words mean?
- Do some of them mean more than one thing? Which ones?

UNIT Vocabulary

u for / ŭ /

brush	crutch	hum	muffin	stunt
bud	cub	hunt	must	such
bug	cup	hush	nut	suffix
bulb	cut	hut	plum	sum
bulk	drug	input	plus	sun
bump	drum	instruct	publish	thus
bun	duck	jug	puff	truck
bunch	dug	jump	pup	trunk
bunk	dump	junk	rug	tug
bus	dust	just	run	until
but	flunk	luck	rush	up
buzz	fun	lunch	rust	upon
catsup	fund	lung	scrub	us
chipmunk	gum	much	skunk	
crust	gun	mud	snug	

u for / o͝o / as in book

bull	bush	full	pull	push	put

o for / ŭ /

come	glove	none	shove	somewhere
done	income	nothing	some	son
from	love	once	someone	ton
front	month	one	something	

Word Relationships

Word Relationships	What Is It?	Unit 9 Examples
antonyms	Words that have opposite meanings	son/daughter; push/pull; plus/minus
synonyms	Words that have the same or similar meaning	cut/trim; luck/fortune; flunk/fail
homophones	Words that sound the same but have different meanings	son/sun; some/sum; one/won
attributes	Words that tell more about other words, such as size, parts, color, and function	grapes/bunch; bee/buzz; duck/quack

Meaning Parts

Review: Adding endings to nouns signals plural or possessive.

-s	Adding **-s** to most singular nouns makes them plural. Example: bugs
-es	Adding **-es** to singular nouns ending in <u>s</u>, <u>z</u>, <u>x</u>, <u>ch</u>, <u>sh</u>, or <u>tch</u> makes them plural. Examples: dresses, fizzes, suffixes, lunches, bushes, matches
-'s	Adding **-'s** to a singular noun makes it possessive. Example: a bug's body

Review: Adding endings to verbs signals number and tense (time).

-s or -es	Adding **-s** or **-es** signals third person singular, present tense. Examples: scrubs, buzzes
-ing	With *am*, *is*, or *are*, adding **-ing** signals present progressive. Examples: am jumping; is rushing; are buzzing
-ed	Adding **-ed** signals past tense. Examples: bumped, scrubbed, hunted

■ Adding **-ing** to verbs used with *was* or *were* signals past progressive.

> **Past Progressive**
>
> **was** push**ing**, **were** push**ing**

STEP 4

Grammar and Usage

Verb Phrases

A **verb phrase** is a group of words that:

- Does the job of a verb
- Conveys tense
- Has two parts: **helping verb (HV)** + **main verb (MV)**

> **Verb Phrase**
>
> HV MV + -ing
> The bus is stopping.
>
> *is* = helping verb
> *stopping* = main verb + **-ing**

Action verbs sometimes have helping verbs. *Am, is, are, was,* and *were* can be used as helping verbs with action verbs.

Past Progressive Verbs

Review: Verbs describe actions. Verbs also show time. If the action happened yesterday, the verb is usually in the **past tense**. Add **-ed** to create regular past tense verb forms. Example: pushed

- The ending **-ing** can also be used with the helping verbs *was* and *were* to signal past progressive. Progressive means an ongoing action.

> **Past Progressive**
> He **was pushing**. They **were pushing**.

Tense Timeline

Yesterday	Today	Tomorrow
Past	Present	Future
-ed	am/is/are + verb + **-ing**	
was/were + verb + **-ing**		

These action verbs can take **-ing**.

Unit 9 Verbs

bluff	cut	instruct	rush
blush	drum	jump	scrub
brush	duck	pump	tug
bump	flunk	push	
buzz	hunt	run	

Irregular Past Tense Verbs

Review: Some verbs signal past time through irregular verb forms. These Unit 9 verbs have irregular past tense forms.

Verbs (Irregular)

Base Verb	Irregular Past Tense	Base Verb	Irregular Past Tense
come	came	put	put
cut	cut	run	ran

Compound Direct Objects

■ A **compound direct object** is two direct objects joined by a conjunction.

> **Compound Direct Object**
>
> The bugs infest *crops.*
>
> The bugs infest *animals.*
>
> The bugs infest *crops* **and** *animals.*

The direct objects, *crops* and *animals,* are joined by the conjunction **and** to build a compound direct object.

The diagram below shows the compound direct object in this sentence.

Form:	N/V/N + N	**noun/verb/noun + noun**
Function:	S/P/DO + DO	**subject/predicate/direct object + direct object**

The bugs infest crops and animals.

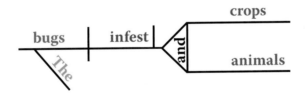

Listening and Reading Comprehension

Informational and Narrative Text

■ Some **informational** text is organized by **classification**. This text includes ideas, facts, evidence, or examples organized into categories. **Transition words** signal this organization.

> **Transition Words for Classification**
>
> the first kind, the second kind, the last kind
>
> one type, another type, a final type
>
> one reason, the next reason, another reason

■ **Narrative** text tells a story. When we read a story, we listen or look for the parts of a story: characters, setting, events, and resolution.

Context Clues

■ **Context clues** help us understand new vocabulary. Pronoun referents, meaning signals, and visuals, such as pictures, charts, and graphs, provide meaning links.

Signal Words

■ Some sentences ask us to remember information from what we have read or heard. Other sentences ask us to read or listen, and then put information together to build meaning. These sentences ask us to **Understand It**. They use specific **signal words**.

> **Signal Words for Understand It**
>
> predict, conclude, illustrate, define in your own words, tell

6 Speaking and Writing

We use different types of sentences when we speak and write.

Statements: Fact or Opinion

- Some sentences present facts or opinions. These are called **statements**.

> **Statements**
>
> **A bug's body has three segments.**
> This tells us a fact about bugs.
>
> What? The body of a bug has three segments.
>
> **All bugs are annoying.**
> This expresses an opinion about bugs.
>
> What? All of them are annoying.

Signal Words

- Some sentences ask for information. They require retrieving information from memory to provide an answer. They use specific **signal words**.

> **Signal Words for Understand It**
>
> **Predict** what could happen if one student came to school with lice.
>
> What do you **conclude** about the effect of eyelash mites?
>
> **Illustrate** the body of a bug.
>
> **Define** bacteria **in your own words**.
>
> **Tell** how dust mites can make us sick.

Paragraph Organization

- Some paragraphs are organized by **classification**, or categories. These paragraphs include ideas, facts, evidence, or examples organized by categories. **Transition words** signal this organization. Examples: one reason, the next reason, the best reason

More About Words

■ **Bonus Words** use the same sound-spelling correspondences that we have studied in Unit 9 and previous units.

■ **Idioms** are common phrases that cannot be understood by the meanings of their separate words—only by the entire phrase.

■ **Word History** tells why some English words use **o** to spell / ŭ /, as in *from*.

UNIT Bonus Words

bathtub	discuss	gut	plug	slum
bluff	disgust	huff	public	spun
blunt	disrupt	hug	pug	stinkbug
blush	dove	hull	pulp	stub
buck	drunk	humbug	pulpit	stuck
bulldog	duct	hump	pump	stud
bust	dud	hunch	pun	stuff
butt	dull	hunchback	punch	stump
checkup	dusk	hung	punk	submit
chestnut	fluff	hunk	putt	suds
chuck	flung	lump	rub	summit
chum	flush	monk	ruff	sung
chunk	flux	mug	rump	sunk
club	fuss	mum	rung	sunlit
clump	grub	mumps	scum	sunset
clung	gruff	mush	setup	swung
crunch	grunt	mustang	shunt	thump
crush	gulf	mutt	shut	trust
cull	gull	oneself	skulk	tub
cult	gulp	pickup	skull	welcome
cusp	gust	pluck	slug	won

Idioms

Idiom	Meaning
be up a creek	be in a difficult situation
don't bug me	leave me alone
get up on the wrong side of bed	be in a really bad mood
pass the buck	shift responsibility to another person
pull your leg	kid, fool, or trick you
push your luck	expect continued good fortune
put all your eggs in one basket	risk everything all at once
run out of gas	exhaust your energy or enthusiasm
stuck in a rut	stay in a way of living that never changes
(when) push comes to shove	(when) the situation becomes more difficult

 Word History

Using the letter o to spell / ŭ /—English words that use o to spell / ŭ / keep an Old English spelling. Most of the English words with unusual spellings come from Old English. In those days people weren't particular about how they spelled words. Many words changed their pronunciations, but the old spellings remain. Most of the short, ordinary words that we use every day come from Old English (which came from Anglo-Saxon).

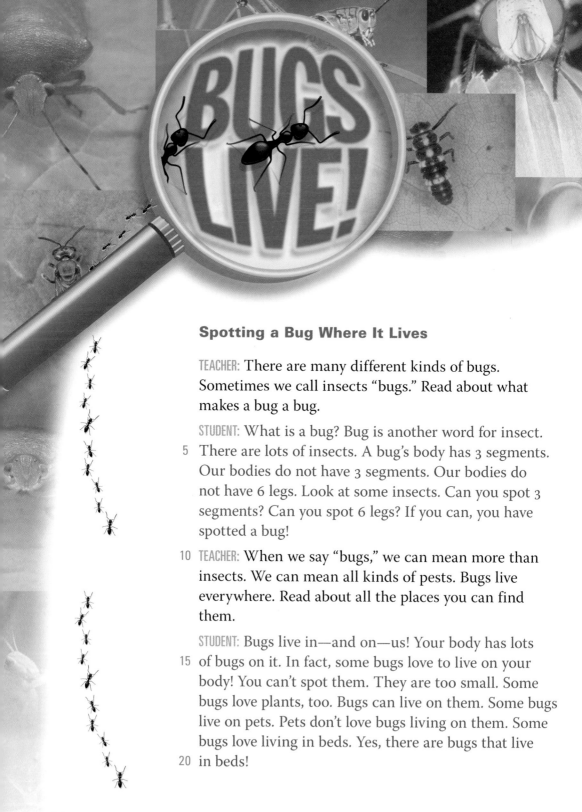

Spotting a Bug Where It Lives

TEACHER: There are many different kinds of bugs. Sometimes we call insects "bugs." Read about what makes a bug a bug.

STUDENT: What is a bug? Bug is another word for insect.
5 There are lots of insects. A bug's body has 3 segments. Our bodies do not have 3 segments. Our bodies do not have 6 legs. Look at some insects. Can you spot 3 segments? Can you spot 6 legs? If you can, you have spotted a bug!

10 TEACHER: When we say "bugs," we can mean more than insects. We can mean all kinds of pests. Bugs live everywhere. Read about all the places you can find them.

STUDENT: Bugs live in—and on—us! Your body has lots
15 of bugs on it. In fact, some bugs love to live on your body! You can't spot them. They are too small. Some bugs love plants, too. Bugs can live on them. Some bugs live on pets. Pets don't love bugs living on them. Some bugs love living in beds. Yes, there are bugs that live
20 in beds!

Dust Mites and Bed Bugs

TEACHER: Learn about some of the invisible bugs that can aggravate allergies.

STUDENT: We fluff the blankets on the bed. Then our eyes get red. We dust the top of the desk. Then our eyes itch.

25 What is happening? Bugs are bugging us. It is not the dust. It's the bugs! To be exact, dust mites are bugging us. You cannot spot a dust mite with your eyes. It is too small. Dust mites live on skin cells that we shed. Some of us get sick from this bug.

30 TEACHER: You'll be shocked to read about the next kind of bug.

STUDENT: Some bugs have wings. Some do not. A bed bug is a wingless bug. Bed bugs are not big. A bed bug is much less than an inch long. How much less? Lots. It

35 is as small as a pencil eraser. It is red. In fact, bed bugs can be called red bugs. Bed bugs are pests. They can hatch up to 200 eggs in a flash. That is a lot of bugs!

The bed bugs live in blankets and mattresses. They could be living in your bed. Then bed bugs chomp on

40 us. They suck blood. Gulp! When we rest in bed, they don't. We get bitten!

Bed bugs live in blankets, mattresses, and pillows.

BAD BUGS

Chinch Bugs

TEACHER: Read about bugs that have an appetite for grass.

STUDENT: Some bugs live in the grass. One such bug is a chinch bug. It is a pest. This bug lives in sod. This pest is bad for grass. Why? When hot months come,
5 chinch bugs drop eggs in the sod. The eggs hatch. Many of the small bugs live. These bugs kill grass. How? They attack grass stems. Then they suck on them. The grass wilts. This kills the grass.

Chinch bugs live in the grass.

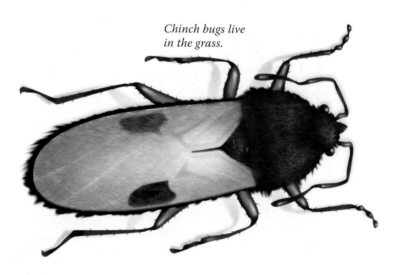

Getting Rid of Bad Bugs

TEACHER: Not only do insects harm our yards, they hurt
10 other plants as well.

STUDENT: **Bugs live on bushes and crops, too. They can
kill them. How? Bugs chomp on the plants' buds and
stems. When these are missing, plants cannot live.
Bugs can transmit sickness as well. This can kill
15 plants. Bugs attack crops and kill them.**

TEACHER: Read about more problems with bugs and
possible solutions.

STUDENT: **Bugs transmit sickness to us. They transmit
sickness to pets and plants, too. Getting rid of bugs
20 is a big job. The task is complex. You have to get to
their nests. They can be anywhere. They are hidden
from us.**

**How do you get rid of bugs? You can give them
something toxic. The toxins will kill them. Think
25 about the impact these toxins have. They kill the bad
bugs. Do they kill helpful bugs as well? What should
we do?**

HOW BUGS BUG US

You've heard this saying: "I've got a bug." You know what it means: "I'm sick." You can't see them, but bugs live all over your body. In fact, you're just a mini-zoo for bugs!

Bugs in Your Bed?

5 Dust mites are one type of bug on your body. Do you wash your pillow? No? If you use the same pillow every night for 10 years, half its weight is from dust mites. You can't see these tiny creatures. Still they are there, feeding on dead skin and sweat. Their droppings
10 cause allergies. They make lots of us sick. Do your eyes sometimes get red and itchy? Does it happen when you shake out the **spread** on your bed? Does it happen when you sweep the floor? Then you're a **victim** of dust mites!

Stomach Alert!

15 Another type of bug that lives on your body is bacteria. Bacteria cover your body, inside and outside. No, you can't see them. They're too small. Most bacteria are not too bad, and some are even good. Bacteria help you **digest** food. Some bad bacteria are called germs. If
20 you don't keep germs in check, they can **spread**. Germs can cause infection and make you sick.

spread
n. a bed covering

victim
one harmed by another

digest
to break down food in the stomach

spread
v. to move over an area

In Your Hair?

The next type of bug that can live on your body is lice. Hair lice just love nice, clean hair. There, they can **hunker** down and **guzzle** blood from the **scalp**.
25 They lay eggs on hair. Lice spread quickly! They spread from head to head. They spread when we work together closely, in school classrooms and at work. If we get lice, special shampoo can get rid of them.

Eyelash Horrors!

Eyelash mites are the final type of bug that exists
30 on our body. You have mites in your eyelashes. Don't worry; they're harmless. These tiny bugs cling to eyelashes with eight tiny legs. They live on sebum, a natural oil in skin and hair. The truth is, lots of bugs just love our skin and hair!

Adapted from *Info Adventure: Amazing Body Science*, with permission of Creative Publishing, Intl.

hunker
to settle down; to stay put

guzzle
to drink very fast

scalp
the skin on top of the head

Lice live in hair.

Eyelash mites live in eyelashes.

Answer It
Say each answer in a complete sentence.

1. Tell how dust mites can make us sick.

2. Define the word bacteria in your own words.

3. Predict what could happen if one student comes to class with lice.

4. What do you conclude about the effect of eyelash mites?

5. Illustrate one type of bug that bugs us. Be sure to label the illustration.

NEW OLD INSECTS

In 2002, new old insects were found. Why were they new? They had not been seen before. Why were they old? They lived a long, long time ago. They are a new order of old insects.

biologists
people who study
living things

5   **Biologists** group living things into orders and species. An order of plants is related. An order of animals is related. All roses are in one order. All frogs are in one order. But there can be many species in one order.

For many years, biologists have sorted all living
10   things into orders. This job has been a lot of work. There are many orders. Millions of living things are in the orders. Some biologists spend their lives on just one order. Some just study insects.

Oliver Zompro is an entomologist. He is a scientist
15   who studies insects. He comes from Germany. Zompro loves insects. People send him chunks of amber. Why do they send him amber? Amber is full of ancient insects. Amber
20   comes from ancient resin. Resin is a gum that drips from trees and covers insects. Millions of years pass. The resin hardens. It becomes
25   hard as stone. Amber can be yellow. It can be gold. It can

Ancient Gladiator trapped in amber.

be brown. Why does Zompro study amber? It is full of insect fossils.

A few years ago, Zompro was looking at a chunk of
30 amber that appeared to be 40 million years old. In the amber were insect fossils. There was something **odd** about it. One of the fossils was not from any order. "This reminds me of something," he thought. "Haven't I seen this insect before?" Then, Zompro remembered.
35 He had been in London, England. In a museum there, he had seen a strange insect. He had also seen a similar insect in a **Berlin** museum. Zompro knew these strange insects were related. They were related to the insect in the ancient amber. These insects were not
40 in any book. Where did they belong in the orders of insects? Where had they come from? Were any insects of this order still living?

Months after that, some entomologists went on a trip to Namibia, in southern Africa. There, they
45 looked for unusual insects. They hit pay dirt! They found living insects that were like the ancient insect Zompro had seen in his chunk of amber! The scientists were **stunned**! They had found a new order! It was big
50 news in science. It was fantastic! This was the first new order of insects in 87 years!

odd
strange or unusual

Berlin
the capital city of Germany

stunned
surprised or shocked

Living Gladiator found in Namibia.

NAMIBIA

predators

living things that kill and eat other living things

antennae

thread-like feelers on the heads of some animals

The new order of insects is called *mantophasmatodea* (pronounced 'măn-tə 'făz-mə 'tō-dē-ə). These insects
55 have a nickname: Gladiators. They look like other insects, such as the walking stick or the praying mantis. But they are **predators**. They have long **antennae**, sharp jaws, and three small teeth. Until this time, they were unknown. There had been no books on these
60 insects. Now they are recorded! They are a new order! They are new old insects!

Answer It
Say each answer in a complete sentence.

1. Who is Oliver Zompro?

2. What did he discover in the chunk of amber?

3. When was a new order of insects found?

4. Where was the discovery made?

5. Tell why you think this discovery was important.

WOW! I'VE JUST FOUND A MOST INTERESTING LITTLE INSECT!

Say "bug," and just about everybody knows exactly what you're talking about. You're talking about one of those tiny six-legged creatures. Or are you? Sometimes, you have to **consider** the context; that is, all the other
5   words *around* a word you're studying. As you think about the following sentences, consider the context around the word bug.

consider
to think about

1. I think she's caught a bug; she hasn't been feeling well all week.
10   2. There must be a bug in the directions, because I can't get this to work. My friend had the same problem when he bought this kit a couple of weeks ago.
3. The newspaper report said that the governor's
15   office had been bugged. They don't know who put the bug in his office, but there is an investigation going on.

Words and Meanings

In any language, a word may have more than one meaning. In English, for example, words often have
20 many meanings. Consider the word **bug**.

Bug can mean many things (nouns):
1. a six-legged insect
2. any small pest
3. a bacteria or virus that causes sickness
25 4. a defect or problem in the way something is designed
5. a computer virus
6. an obsession (She has a golf *bug*.)
7. a tiny electronic device, hidden for secret
30 listening.

Those meanings are just for the *noun* **bug**! How about **bug** as a *verb*?
1. get bigger (Their eyes will **bug out** when they see the car.)
35 2. annoy, pester (They like to **bug** the teacher about it.)
3. worry (That story will **bug** me until I find out the truth.)
4. equip with an electronic listening device (Did
40 someone **bug** the office?)

Formal and Informal Language

There are many kinds of language; mostly, they can be divided into formal language and informal language. Formal English is often called *academic English*. It is the language of textbooks. To succeed in
45 school and work, we have to learn academic English. But in **casual**, everyday conversation, people often communicate in more informal language. Some informal language is *slang*. Slang is language that is casual and playful. A slang **expression** can consist of
50 a single word, a phrase, or a whole conversation. Slang often contains words that are substitutes for more

casual
relaxed; not formal

expression
a saying; a particular way of saying things

formal words. Many slang expressions mean something very different from what is actually said. Slang is very different from academic English.

55 Several English slang expressions use the word **bug**. The following are two slang examples of **bug**.

bug off: To leave someone alone. (We told them to **bug off**.)

bug out: 1. To leave or quit, usually in a hurry.
60 (Sorry, but I've got to **bug out** of here.)
2. To **avoid** a duty or responsibility; to desert. (They **bugged out** on us.)

avoid
to stay away from

How about more to bug you? This time, it's a dose of

BUGGY IDIOMS

Match these six idiomatic expressions with their meanings. (Find the answers at the end.)

Idioms	Meanings
1. be as snug as a bug in a rug	A. share the same interest or hobby
2. don't let the bed bugs bite	B. be as comfortable as possible
3. bitten by the same bug	C. told me about it secretly
4. put a bug in my ear	D. leave me alone
5. don't bug me	E. isn't normal or sane
6. be crazy as a june bug	F. watch out for yourself; be careful

answers: 1.B 2.F 3.A 4.C 5.D 6.E

Geography Bugs?

Oh yes, there's more! There are even **bugs** in geography. There's the **Bug River**. The Bug has two
65 main arteries: one, the Western Bug, flows through Eastern Europe, from **Ukraine** through Poland. The other, the Southern Bug, runs from Ukraine into the Black Sea.

Ukraine
a country in
Eastern Europe

It's in the Context

The next time you think you **comprehend** the
70 meaning of a word, take a minute to think about it. Listen or read carefully, and always consider the context. Clues to the meaning are often in the context. If the use of a word is not familiar to you, use a dictionary at home or in your classroom. A little work
75 just might take some of the **bugs** out of reading!

comprehend
to understand

*The Western Bug River
flows from Ukraine
through Poland.*

Think About It

1. Explain the meaning of the word context.

2. List three meanings for the word bug.

3. English words can have many different meanings. How does this make English difficult to learn and understand?

4. What is the difference between formal language and informal language? Find the answer in your text.

5. Choose your favorite "buggy" idiom. Describe why it is your favorite.

6. Why do you think it is so important to consider the context when you read?

LIGHTING BUGS

A bunch of us were hanging around after school for practice. Our school was getting ready for a big holiday **program** . We put on a fabulous show every year, and this year I was in charge of the lighting. I guess the
5   music director thought I could do the job. Everybody knows I'm into computers, plus I've got these two friends, André and Nela; they're into computers, too. Some people might think we're geeks, but we have a lot of fun. Really. We just like learning about what
10 computers can do.

   We had been practicing for over a month, so the choir and band were pretty much ready. These kids are tremendous talents. I'm not just bragging about our school, but we have some amazing musicians. Now me,
15 I'm not musical, so I never was in any of those groups. But the computer I like. I started when I was a little kid, and I guess I was just a natural.

   Anyway, we had rehearsed the show so many times that I felt like I was managing the lighting controls
20 in my sleep. I had **programmed** the lights in our

> **program**
> *n.* a performance

> **programmed**
> *v.* set up a machine to perform specific acts

auditorium to go up gradually. When the choir first walked in, holding candles and singing, the only light came from the candles they held. Then, as they walked from the back to the front of the auditorium, the band
25 started playing, and the choir started to sing. The stage lights slowly went up, and the colors changed from red to green to blue. When the entire choir was on the stage, they blew their candles out, and the full stage lighting was on. I never told anybody this, but it sent
30 chills up and down my spine. Really. It was just one of those very cool moments.

I had programmed lots of awesome lighting. Spotlights **automatically** lit up the soloists, so when different acts came on, the lights would focus on
35 them. Sometimes, lights moved around while the acts performed. We had synchronized the lights, so they automatically changed color, dimmed, and re-intensified. The effect was amazing—and it was all programmed in my laptop, so all I had to do was to
40 take **cues** from the music. It was a snap.

Well, let me get back to my story. We were backstage, working out our final run-through before **dress rehearsal**. There's this girl named Kim Wong in our class, and she has an incredibly beautiful voice.
45 Just when Kim approached the top platform, I clicked for the next lighting change. Blue spots would light her, and then the lights would change again, just like we had done dozens of times before. I had also programmed the lights to suggest falling snow, but the blue spotlight
50 didn't hit Kim; it didn't look like snow. Instead, the entire auditorium went dark. Everybody screamed, and some people were really scared. Some guys helped Kim get down, but it was extremely chaotic. Then I heard the director yelling my name. My laptop gave off a little
55 light because it was running on the battery, so I tried to get into the **program** and fix it quickly. I had no luck, though; my lighting program was frozen.

automatically
self-operating; working by itself

cues
signals showing when to start an action

dress rehearsal
the final practice before a perfor-mance

program
n. a set of coded instructions that tell a computer to perform a task

It took 45 minutes or so for the music director to totally evacuate the auditorium. He told everybody
60 to go home until the next day's dress rehearsal and evening performance. We just had to figure out what had caused my lighting program to freeze. I knew everybody thought I was crazy, especially when we'd practiced the program so many times before.

65   I was starting to get panicky. Everybody in the program was counting on me. So I went over to André's house; Nela was there, too. "Look at this awesome game we're downloading," André shouted. We liked to download games from the Internet. That way, we could
70 play games from each other's houses. They wanted me to get into the new game right then.

    "I'll do the download, but then I need help. My lighting program froze; I mean, the entire rehearsal had to shut down and everybody had to go home. Really."
75   "So where's your **backup** ?" Nela asked.

    "Don't ask," I told her. I hadn't created a backup disk; I was so confident about my program that I'd never made one. They glanced at each other and shook their heads. But they're my friends, so I knew they'd

Note the storyteller's repeated use of **really**.

Do you repeat the same word or phrase too often when you talk?

Do you have any friends who do this? What words or phrases do they repeat?

backup

n. a copy of a program or file that is stored separately from the original

80 try to help me. The three of us concentrated on the
lighting program for about six hours that evening. We
did everything we could think of. We walked over to
the computer store and talked to an expert in repairs.
Nada. He said everything appeared flawless. The laptop
85 worked, but the lighting program was frozen. It had
to be some kind of bug, but he didn't have a clue what
kind. I called my mom and told her I couldn't come
home until we could find the bug and get rid of it. A
lighting bug: that's what I told her it was. But we never
90 could run the program, and about 9:00 P.M., Nela said
she had to go home. Andre had to do some chores for
his mom, so I headed home, too.

That night I had a hard time falling asleep,
imagining various scenarios with the lights. The dress
95 rehearsal was tomorrow afternoon, and the holiday
production was tomorrow night! And I had to go back
there and tell everyone that I couldn't fix it. Plus, I
hadn't **backed up** the lighting program. That was
the most incredibly dumb mistake in the whole world.
100 Really. No backup; that was really stupid.

FATAL
ERROR

backed up

v. copied a computer
file or program to
have a copy of the
original

Eventually I must have fallen asleep, because the next thing I knew, my mom was yelling at me and telling me it was time to get dressed for school. Before I even opened my eyes, though, I thought about my

105 laptop. I couldn't imagine how I could face everybody. How could I face the music teachers? They had put in so many months of hard work and planning! I wanted to disappear. I didn't want to go to school; I actually thought about staying home. But then, I thought,

110 "Maybe something will happen. Maybe we can get it fixed. Besides, everybody will be even madder at me if I don't show up today." So I got dressed and **trudged** down the steps with my laptop. The laptop didn't weigh much, but the lighting bug I carried was heavy.

115   When I got outside, I saw Nela waiting for me on the corner where we always meet. When she saw me she was very excited, and she shouted at me, "I think I've figured it out! It was that game! That's where you got the bug. Get rid of the game, and we'll get rid of the

120 bug, I promise you!"

    "That can't be it!" I answered, approaching her. "The program had shut down before I even went over to André's house yesterday afternoon."

    "No! No!" Nela was all excited, "I remembered

125 something when I woke up this morning. Way last week, remember? We all tried to download that one complicated game; André and I tried it, but we couldn't get it to download. It only worked on your laptop, remember?" As I thought about it, it made sense.

130 Maybe deleting that game from my laptop would get rid of the bug. Maybe the lighting bug would be squished; maybe we'd get lucky.

    As soon as we got to school, we located André. There wasn't time to do anything then because the bell

135 was about to ring, but Nela told him, "We'll see you at lunch. We think we have the problem fixed!" We'd only have 45 minutes to try to delete the game and test the

> What does the storyteller mean when he says, "The laptop didn't weigh much, but the lighting bug I carried was heavy"?

trudged
walked with difficulty

lighting program. Dress rehearsal was scheduled for 1:30 that afternoon.

140   Right after the bell rang, the music director called me out of science class. "I *know* you got that program fixed," he demanded in his sternest voice. "This is the most important event we present during the entire school year, and your classmates have worked hard."

145 Like I didn't know that already. So I promised him everything would be fine, no sweat. (Well, the problem wasn't quite fixed, but at least we had an idea where we could begin.) We just knew we had to fix it before the dress rehearsal. All morning long, kids kept coming

150 up to me and asking about it, and I tried to act as if we had it under control.

        Nela's hunch paid off. During lunch period, we deleted the buggy game from my laptop and restarted the lighting program. We even made a backup of

155 the entire program (a little late, I know). Despite my agonizing, the lighting program worked fine during the dress rehearsal. But I was still crazy with worry. You can delete whatever application or document brings a bug into your computer, but the bug still can infect

160 other parts of your computer. It can get into your hard drive. That's why they call it a bug, I guess. I thought everything would probably be fine for the performance, but what if it wasn't? I would look like a total idiot. Really.

165   It was a cold winter night for the performance. As a huge crowd plowed into our school auditorium, I overheard one lady saying, "I hope that careless boy got the lights fixed. Seems like these kids nowadays don't take anything seriously." Can you imagine how I felt?

170 Everybody's families and friends had come to see the singers and musicians on their big night. The crowd was buzzing, and I just knew they were all wondering if the "careless boy's" lights would go out again.

It was showtime. The music director signaled,
175 "Begin," and he gave the choir their cue. They started
filing into the auditorium with their lighted candles,
singing. The audience was completely quiet. It was
beautiful. Really. Now it was time for the lights to
come on. My heart was beating so hard I could hear it
180 in my ears. I was that nervous.

My laptop was ready, and the program was
running; just one click from me, and there would be
light. I took a deep breath and clicked. As the choir
walked from the back to the front of the auditorium,
185 the stage lights gradually grew brighter, until they
went full up. When everybody was on stage, I clicked
again. They blew their candles out, and the full stage
lighting went on. This was just the way it was supposed
to work. After they finished singing, the first soloist
190 stepped out. I clicked again, and the spotlights hit him
perfectly as he began to sing. Everyone in the audience
clapped; it was like a miracle.

The rest of the show went like clockwork. The
kids all did a wonderful job, and the lighting was
195 spectacular. You know, the singers and musicians
at our school are really fabulous. I do have to say,
though, the show was even more awesome,
thanks to my lighting program. Really.

Think About It

1. What part of the performance was the narrator's responsibility?

2. Describe the lighting at the beginning of the performance.

3. Do you think the storyteller was proud of the lighting program? How do you know this? Cite places in the text that defend your answer.

4. When a story has a narrator, the story has a *voice*, a personality. Describe the storyteller. Explain your answer.

5. Why do you think the storyteller failed to make a backup of the lighting program? Think of a time when someone had to do something but failed to do it. What was the result?

6. The title of this story, "Lighting Bugs," is a play on words. What familiar phrase is pronounced very much like "lighting bugs"? Define each phrase in your own words.

Unit 10

Take Time

STEP 1

Phonemic Awareness and Phonics

Unit 10 introduces the long vowel sounds: / ā /, / ē /, / ī /, / ō /, and / ō͞o /.

Vowels

- The long vowel sound for **a**, **e**, **i**, and **o** is the same as the name of the letter that represents it.

  / ā /   as in **make**

  / ē /   as in **these**

  / ī /   as in **time**

  / ō /   as in **vote**

- The long vowel sound for **u** can be pronounced two ways.

  / ō͞o / as in **tube**;   / yō͞o / as in **cute**

The diacritical mark for the long vowel sound is the macron (¯): ā, ē, ī, ō, and ō͞o.

Go to the **Vowel Chart** on page 204. Find the five long vowel sounds and these example words on the chart: **make**, **these**, **time**, **vote**, and **tube**.

STEP

2

Word Recognition and Spelling

Using Unit 10 sound-spelling correspondences, we can read and spell words like these unit words: **made, Pete, pine, rode, tube, use**.

■ These **CVC** words change when **e** is added at the end.

VC + Final e

mad — made

pet — Pete

pin — pine

rod — rode

tub — tube

us — use

1. The vowel sound changes from a short vowel to a long vowel.

2. The final **e** is silent.

■ This is called the **vowel + consonant + e** pattern, or **final silent e**. The **e** at the end of the word is a signal to use the long vowel sound. The final **e** is silent.

Spelling Rule: Drop e

■ When adding a suffix to a **final silent e** word:

1. If the suffix begins with a vowel, drop the **e** from the base word.

> **Drop e Rule**
>
> Adding a suffix with a vowel:
>
> hope + ing = hoping

2. If the suffix begins with a consonant, do not drop the **e** from the base word.

> **Drop e Rule**
>
> Adding a suffix with a consonant:
>
> hope + ful = hopeful

Contractions

Review: **Contractions** are two words combined into one word. Some letters are left out and are replaced by an apostrophe. In Unit 10, the contractions are made with the word **will**.

> **Contraction With Will**
>
> I + **will** = **I'll**
>
> The letters **wi** in **will** are replaced with an apostrophe (').

> ### Unit 10 Contractions
>
> | I'll | we'll |
> |------|-------|
> | you'll | you'll |
> | he'll, she'll, it'll | they'll |

Unit 10 Essential Words

almost	already	although
alone	also	always

Spelling Lists

The Unit 10 spelling lists contain three word categories:

1. Words with the long vowels spelled **vowel** + **consonant** + <u>e</u>
2. **Essential Words** (in italics)
3. Contractions with **will** spelled **'ll**

Spelling Lists

Lessons 1–5

almost	hole
alone	joke
already	ride
also	rules
although	theme
always	these
bake	time
game	

Lessons 6–10

base	ropes
cave	shapes
faded	size
I'll	they'll
lake	voting
lined	white
live	you'll
nine	

Vocabulary and Morphology

Unit Vocabulary

Sound-spelling correspondences from Unit 10 and previous units make up the unit vocabulary.

- What do these words mean?
- Do some of them mean more than one thing? Which ones?

UNIT Vocabulary

Final silent e

ape	game	made	ride	sole
bake	gate	make	ripe	take
base	gave	mane	rise	tame
bike	hate	mate	rope	tape
cake	hike	mile	rose	theme
came	hive	mine	rote	these
case	hole	mode	rule	those
cave	home	mule	safe	time
chase	hope	name	sale	tone
choke	hose	nine	same	tube
cone	joke	nose	save	use
date	lake	note	shade	vase
dime	lane	pave	shake	vote
dine	late	pile	shape	wake
dive	life	pine	shave	wave
fade	like	pipe	shine	white
file	line	pole	side	wide
fine	live	quite	site	wife
five	lone	quote	size	wipe

Word Relationships

Word Relationships	What Is It?	Unit 10 Examples
antonyms	Words that have opposite meanings	give/take; hate/love; late/early
synonyms	Words that have the same or similar meaning	dine/eat; hope/wish; safe/secure
homophones	Words that sound the same but have different meanings	hole/whole; passed/past
attributes	Words that tell more about other words such as size, parts, color, and function	bike/rim; sun/shine; tree/pine

Meaning Parts

Review: Adding endings to verbs signals number and tense (time).

-s or **-es**	Adding -**s** or -**es** signals third person singular, present tense. Examples: dives, crunches
-ed	Adding -**ed** means past tense. Example: chased
-ing	Adding -**ing** means present progressive when used with *am*, *is*, or *are*. Examples: am chasing, is diving, are hoping
-ing	Adding -**ing** means past progressive when used with *was* or *were*. Examples: was chasing; were diving

Grammar and Usage

Common and Proper Nouns

■ A **common noun** names a general person, place, or thing. Examples: woman, mountain, clock

■ A **proper noun** names a specific person, place, or thing. Examples: Mrs. Jones, White Mountains, Big Ben

Concrete and Abstract Nouns

■ A **concrete noun** names a person, place, or thing that we can see or touch. Examples: girl, cave, cake

■ An **abstract noun** names an idea or a thought that we cannot see or touch. Examples: hate, Sunday, hope

Nouns can be subjects or direct objects in sentences. His **wife** gave the **cake** to him. (wife = subject; cake = direct object)

Unit 10 Nouns

base	dome	joke	maze	side
bone	fame	kite	note	tale
cake	file	lake	pine	tape
cave	five	life	pope	tile
code	haze	lime	robe	time
date	hope	male	safe	vine

Future Tense

Review: A **phrase** is a group of words that does the same job as a single word. In the sentence: The dog is sitting, *is sitting* is a **verb phrase**.

■ A verb phrase can convey **future time**.

> **Future Verb Phrases**
>
> The cat **will nap**.
>
> In this sentence, *will nap* is a verb phrase that refers to the future. The verb *will* signals future tense.

Tense Timeline

Yesterday	Today	Tomorrow
Past	Present	Future
		will

Unit 10 Verbs

Base Verb	Future Tense	Base Verb	Future Tense
chase	will chase	name	will name
hope	will hope	ride	will ride
make	will make	shake	will shake

Irregular Past Tense Verbs

Review: Some verbs show past time with irregular verb forms.

Unit 10 Verbs (Irregular)

Base Verb	Irregular Past Tense	Base Verb	Irregular Past Tense
dive	dove	shake	shook
make	made	shine	shone
ride	rode	take	took
rise	rose	wake	woke

Compound Sentences

Review: Any part of a sentence can be compounded. The compound parts—compound subjects, predicates, or direct objects—are joined by a coordinating conjunction, such as **and**:

Subjects: *Jules **and** Dan* fed the animals.

Predicates: Jules *fed **and** watched* the animals.

Direct objects: Jules fed *the fish **and** animals*.

■ **A compound sentence** is two sentences joined by a conjunction.

> **Compound Sentence With and**
>
> Julio walked.
>
> Dan ran.
>
> Julio walked **and** Dan ran.

In this compound sentence, *Julio walked* and *Dan ran* are joined by the conjunction **and**.

The diagram below shows how to build this compound sentence with two base sentences.

Form:　　N/V + N/V　**noun/verb + noun/verb**
Function:　S/P + S/P　**subject/predicate + subject/predicate**

Nguyen swims and his brother dives.

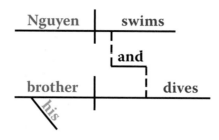

Listening and Reading Comprehension

Informational and Narrative Text

■ Some **informational** text is organized by **time sequence**. This text includes ideas, facts, evidence, or examples organized into categories. **Transition words** signal this organization.

> **Transition Words for Time Sequence**
> first, next, last
> in the beginning, then, later, finally
> yesterday, today, tomorrow

■ **Narrative** text tells a story. When we read a story, we listen or look for the parts of a story: characters, setting, events, and resolution.

Context Clues

■ **Context clues** help us understand new vocabulary. Pronoun referents, meaning signals, and visuals, such as pictures, charts, and graphs, provide meaning links.

Signal Words

■ Some sentences ask us to remember information from what we have read or heard. Other sentences ask us to read or listen, and then put information together to build meaning. These sentences ask us to **Understand It**. They use specific **signal words**.

> **Signal Words for Understand It**
> summarize, identify, paraphrase

STEP 6

Speaking and Writing

We use different types of sentences when we speak and write.

Statements: Fact or Opinion

■ Some sentences present facts or opinions. These are called **statements**.

> **Statements**
>
> **A clock tells time.**
>
> > This tells us a fact about the clock.
> >
> > What? It tells time.
>
> **Time goes by too quickly on weekends.**
>
> > This expresses an opinion about time.
> >
> > What? It goes by too quickly on weekends.

Signal Words

■ Some sentences ask for information. They require putting information or ideas together to create an answer. They use specific **signal words**.

> **Signal Words for Understand It**
>
> **Summarize** the ways to tell time.
>
> **Identify** two parts of a mechanical clock.
>
> **Paraphrase** how scientists decided where time zones would begin.

Paragraph Organization

■ Some paragraphs are organized by **time sequence**. The content of these paragraphs includes ideas, facts, evidence, or examples organized in a sequence. **Transition words** signal this organization. Examples: first, next, last

More About Words

- **Bonus Words** use the same sound-spelling correspondences that we have studied in this unit and previous units.

- **Idioms** are common phrases that cannot be understood by the meanings of their separate words—only by the entire phrase.

- **Word History** tells why English has two words for *time*.

UNIT Bonus Words

ale	fame	lobe	rave	tile
ate	fate	male	rite	tune
bale	faze	maze	robe	twine
bite	flake	mime	rode	vane
bone	fume	mole	role	vile
cane	gale	mute	rude	vine
cave-in	gaze	off-line	sake	wade
chime	glade	offspring	sane	wane
chose	grime	online	shale	whale
code	gripe	pale	shame	while
coke	hale	pane	shone	whine
cope	haze	pike	shrine	woke
cove	hide	plume	slate	wove
cute	jade	poke	slime	yoke
daze	jive	pope	slope	yule
dome	jute	pose	spine	zone
dude	kite	prime	spite	
duke	lame	quake	stripe	
eve	lime	rake	tale	
fake	lineup	rate	tide	

Idioms	
Idiom	**Meaning**
be at the end of your rope	be at the limit of one's patience, endurance, or resources
bite the dust	fall dead, especially in combat; be defeated; come to an end
come up smelling like a rose	result favorably or successfully
go down the tubes	fall into a state of failure or ruin
make a dent in	get started with a series of chores
rub your nose in it	remind you of something unfortunate that has happened
shake a leg	hurry
take a hike	leave because your presence is unwanted
take a stand	take an active role in demonstrating your belief in something
take it from the top	start from the beginning

 **Word History**

Tense—Why do we say "future tense" instead of "future time"? In Latin, the word for tense was *tempus*. Then, in Old French, the word became *time*. Later, the English borrowed the Middle French word for *time*, but used their own Middle English word, *tens*, to refer to time in language. Today, Modern English speakers use two different words to mean the same thing.

Past Time

Time is passing. How can we tell? The sun shines on us. Our planet moves. Time passes. We track time as our planet moves. This is the basis for time.

5   Think of the past. People made things to track time. They stuck a stick in the sand. The stick's shade moved. It moved as our planet did. Our planet spun in space. The shade moved. Time passed. The shade shifted.

10   Next, came sundials. Sundials tracked the sun's shade. How? An object with three sides sat on the sundial. It cast the shade in an exact spot. It let people guess the time. That was fine if the sun was out. What if it was not? They made candles. They made notches

15 in the wax. At sunset, people lit them. They lit them at the top. They noted the time passing. The wax melted as time passed. The flame made the wax melt. They watched the candles. They could guess the time for sunrise.

20   An hourglass was not like these things. It had sand inside. The sand inside tracked passing time. Sand moved from the top. It went into a hole. It dropped into the base. Was this time exact? It was not. A long time passed. Then exact clocks came. We take clocks for

25 granted. What was life like without clocks?

By making notches in a candle, people could tell time. A nail inserted at a specific hour would drop as the wax melted away. The sound of the nail dropping acted as an alarm clock.

It's About Time

Where do you live? What time zone is it? The globe has 24 time zones. They are about the same size. Time zone lines run from pole to pole. The continental U.S. has four time zones. You cross from zone to zone. You
5 must adjust the clock. Set the time ahead or back an hour. Take a ride. Drive west in the U.S. You drive into the next time zone. Set your clock back 1 hour. You have an extra hour. Drive east. You cross into another time zone. This time you lose an hour. Adjust your clock.
10 Think about planes. Planes can cross many time zones. A plane takes off from Wisconsin. It is 6:00 p.m. It crosses 12 time zones. The plane lands. It is 6:00 a.m.! On that side of the globe, it is the next day! It was a long trip. Your body's clock tells you one time. Check
15 the time in this zone. The times don't match! The clock inside your body is mixed up. You have jet lag! Rest helps. It takes time to adjust.
What time is it? We have 12-hour clocks in our homes. It is 5:00. Is it 5:00 a.m.? Is it 5:00 p.m.? Use a
20 24-hour clock. It can help. With it, 5:00 p.m. is 1700 hours. 5:00 a.m. is 0500 hours. Can you tell time like this? Telling time is quite a skill!

A plane may cross several time zones in one trip. If a plane leaves Wisconsin at 6 p.m. and crosses 12 time zones, when it lands in Omsk, Russia, it's the next day.

TELLING TIME

We have used many ways to tell time. We have used the sun. We have used water. We have used candles. We have used weights and springs. Today, we use atomic particles to tell time.

5   One of the first devices was the sundial. It was used from about 1500 to 1300 BC. The Egyptians measured the time of day. How? They measured the sun's shadow. Days were shorter during the winter. They were longer during the summer. The sun almost always shines in Egypt. This

10   method was a good one for these early people.

    The next method used water to tell time. That happened around 400 BC. Ancient Greeks used this method. They measured the outflow of water from a **vessel**. This water clock measured time.

15   Then, people burned candles to tell time. This happened around the year AD 1000. Two different

> **vessel**
> a hollow container, such as a pitcher, used to hold liquids

method
a regular way of doing something

civilizations had the same idea. Each was far from the other. But they began using the same **method** to tell time. Alfred the Great was a king. He was a Saxon king.
20 He ruled in an area that is now part of England. The Saxons burned candles to tell time. The Sung Dynasty had power in China. They ruled about the same time period. They, too, burned candles to mark time.

Later, during the 1400s, the first mechanical clocks
25 appeared. These were built in Europe. They used a mainspring and balance wheel. Now, telling time relied upon a mechanical device.

physicist
a person who studies matter and energy

Finally, around 1950, we began to use atomic clocks. Isidor Rabi was the first one to think of this idea. He was
30 a **physicist**. His clock was based on the study of **atoms**. Atomic clocks measure the vibration of atoms. By 1967, the way we tell time became even more **precise**. One second was defined. It was 9,192,631,770 vibrations of the cesium atom. In 1999, the latest atomic clock came
35 online. It had even more incredible accuracy. Now everyone around the world measures time the same way.

atoms
the smallest units of an element

Today, telling time does not **vary**.

precise
exact

vary
to show change

Answer It
Say each answer in a complete sentence.

1. When did the Egyptians use the sundial?

2. When was water used to tell time?

3. Identify two civilizations that used candles to tell time.

4. Identify two parts in a mechanical clock.

5. Identify the type of atom used in the most precise atomic clock.

1999—The National Institute of Standards and Technology-F1 Cesium Fountain Clock with developers Steve Jefferts and Dawn Meekhof.

Circa 1955—One of the world's first atomic clocks using cesium atoms as the vibration source.

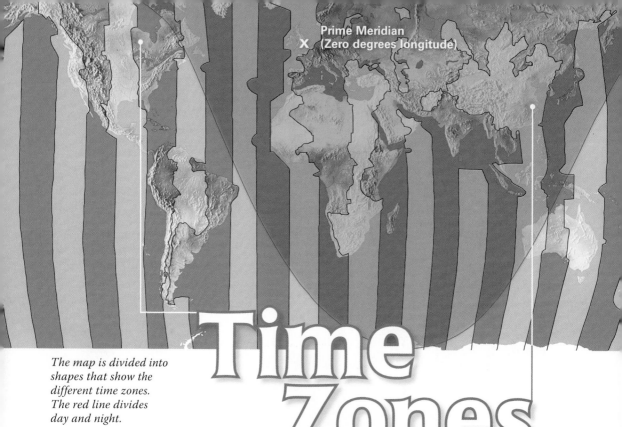

Prime Meridian
X (Zero degrees longitude)

The map is divided into shapes that show the different time zones. The red line divides day and night.

Time Zones

Is it day where you live? If so, it is night on the opposite side of planet Earth. It could also be today or tomorrow. It depends on where you are. Is this confusing? The answer has to do with time **zones**.

5   The Earth is **divided** into time zones. There are 24 different time zones. There is one time zone for each hour. There are 24 hours in a day. That makes 24 different time zones. **Local** times are different all over the world. How did we ever figure it all out? Scientists
10 had to solve some problems. They had to make a worldwide time zone system.

    First, scientists had to decide how to divide up the Earth. They decided to use longitude. Longitude is a system of **imaginary** lines. These lines are shown on
15 globes and maps. They are vertical. They pass through the North and South poles. New time zones begin at about every 15 degrees longitude. See the map above.

zones
areas of land or sky that have a special purpose

divided
split or separated into sections or parts

local
nearby, as in the same town

imaginary
not real; not actually existing

Then, scientists needed to decide where time zones would begin. Which longitude line would be the start point? Scientists chose a **random** longitude line. They called this line the *prime meridian*. This longitude line passes through Greenwich, England. (See the **x** on the map.) It is labeled "zero degrees longitude." Greenwich Mean Time (GMT) **refers** to the time in Greenwich, England. This is the longitudinal start point for all time zones. GMT is also called Universal Time (UT) or Zulu time (Z).

Finally, a 24-hour clock had to be created. Our 12-hour clocks were confusing. People would confuse 3:00 a.m. with 3:00 p.m.! On a 24-hour clock, midnight is 0:00. Noon is 12:00. Think about it this way. It means that 2:00 p.m. is 14:00. See if you can figure this out. What number would be used for 8:00 p.m. on the 24-hour clock? (If you answered 20:00, you're right!)

Now, find the time zone where you live. What time is it? Count 12 time zones to the east. That is to the right. You are on the opposite side of the Earth from where you live. If it is day where you are, it is night there!

random
without purpose or plan; by chance

refers
relates to; means

On the 24-hour clock, midnight is 0:00. Noon is 12:00, so 2:00 p.m. is 14:00.

Answer It
Say each answer in a complete sentence.

1. How many time zones are there?
2. Where in the world do time zones begin?
3. What is the 24-hour clock?
4. Identify two facts about longitude.
5. Paraphrase how scientists decided where time zones would begin.

_____ _____ a/an _____ longitude line.

Creating the Calendar

relied

depended on

In ancient times, people **relied** on the movements of the sun and the moon to predict when certain days would occur. Somebody decided to make a calendar. The question: How would they organize it? How many
5 days should be in a year or a month?

Thousands of years ago, people already understood the concepts of a *month* and a *year*. The lunar cycle (cycle of the moon) lasts 29½ days. That would be the *base calendar* for one month. The solar cycle (cycle
10 of the sun) lasts 365¼ days. That would be the base calendar for one year. But there was a problem. Twelve lunar months (354 days) don't add up to a solar year. It's 11¼ days too short. But adding another lunar month made the solar year 18½ days too long.

15 Why is the lunar cycle important? A lunar calendar measures the time it takes to go from one new moon to the next. A lunar calendar has certain advantages. For one thing, it is always possible to tell the day of the lunar month from the phase of the moon. How? Every
20 month begins with the new moon phase.

However, from a farmer's point of view, the lunar calendar has never been **adequate**. Every agricultural civilization has always followed solar time. Why? The changing position of the sun in the sky determines the
25 seasons. Also, it is the sun—not the moon—that makes things grow. The beginnings and ends of seasons, critical to farmers, are perfectly forecast in a solar calendar.

> **adequate**
>
> enough to meet a need

How Different Civilizations Marked Time on a Calendar

The Egyptians

First came the ancient Egyptian civilization. Many
30 centuries ago, Egyptians were already watching the monthly phases of the moon. They would note the paths of certain stars across a night sky. They noted the position of the sun in the heavens from day to day. These ancient Egyptians realized that they could predict the
35 movements of the moon, the stars, and the sun. Also, they could predict the time of the year that the Nile River would swell with water and flood the land. Soon, the ancient Egyptians came to understand the value of using these observations of the sky as a means for
40 measuring time. To do so, they created several systems. One excellent system matched the movement of heavenly bodies with the flooding of the Nile.

In this system, the Egyptian year (*renpet*) was divided into 12 months (*abed*). Each month had 30 days (*heru*).
45 The year also was divided into three seasons (*ter*). These

A lunar calendar measures the time it takes to go from one new moon to the next.

were four months each, named for the effects of the Nile on the land. The first season was called *akhet*, which means "flood," because the Nile would overflow its banks during this time. The second season was called *perit*, or 50 "emergence," because the floodwaters would **subside** and the farmland seemed to emerge or appear. The final season, *shemu*, "deficiency of water," indicated those months when the Nile was at its lowest point, before the flood came again.

55   In this *renpet* calendar, the 12 months of 30 days each made a year of only 360 days. Although they did not realize that the Earth revolved around the sun, they understood that the cycle of the sun took 365 days and a fraction of a 366th day to complete. Did they create 60 the leap year that we have every four years? Not quite. Instead, they added the *heru renpet*, literally the "five added days," to every year.

THE CHINESE

Next, the Chinese used two calendars. One is a *solar calendar* like ours. It is based on the revolution of the 65 Earth around the sun. The other, which determines many festivals, is the *lunar calendar*. It is based on the movements of the moon.

Long before the Chinese invented ways to trace the sun's yearly movements and created a solar calendar, they 70 used a lunar calendar to set dates for festivals and other events. Every Chinese seasonal festival is connected with some phase of the moon. Often, it is the full moon, which provides bright nights for celebration.

Later in Chinese history, farmers could rely on the 75 skills of astronomers at the imperial court. They had special equipment to calculate the solar cycle. Today, farmers still need to carry out planting and harvesting at the best times. They can buy a book of simple date conversions called the *Wan Nian Li* (10,000-year 80 almanac) or a special almanac called the *Li Shu*. This

subside

to return to a normal level

gives the days in both the solar and lunar cycles, as well as special advice. This book tells a farmer when to cut trees and when to repair the roof. It tells how to cure a twitching eye or how to interpret bad dreams.

85   Each year of the Chinese calendar is associated with one of 12 animals. Each year is the year of one of these: rat, ox, tiger, rabbit, dragon, snake, horse, sheep, monkey,

90   rooster, dog, or pig. These 12 symbols, sometimes called Earthly Branches, combine with the five elements of Chinese traditional science. These are

95   called Heavenly Stems (wood, fire, earth, metal, and water). They form cycles of 60 years (12 times 5). In other words, each year is associated with both an animal and a stem, and every 60 years the

100   same animal and stem are united again. If you were born in 1982, you are a "water dog," while babies born in 1995 are "wood pigs." A 60th birthday is a time for great celebration, since the lucky person has achieved a complete life cycle.

THE ROMANS

105   Then, along came the Roman civilization. The first *Roman calendar* had only 10 months—six months of 30 days and four months of 31. Somebody failed to calculate the math on this one! The Roman calendar came up 61¼ days *short* of the solar year!

龙

Chinese character for "dragon."

110   The bad math quickly caught up with the Romans. Holidays and seasons came at the wrong times. So, Numa, the second king of Rome, made a new calendar. He added 51 days to the year. Because he had extra days, he needed two new months. He added January and
115 February.

Numa's calendar of 355 days was still 10 days too short. So, for lack of a better idea, the Romans added another month, Mercedinus, after February, to balance out the solar year. However, they didn't always remember
120 to do this, so seasons came in the wrong months again. When Julius Caesar ruled Rome, he decided to fix that.

Caesar did some **radical** calendar surgery. He added three months. That gave the year 46 BC 445 days. It was a long year. (The Romans called it "the year of
125 confusion.") But the next year, 45 BC, began in the right season.

To keep things running smoothly, Caesar made the *Julian calendar.* This was a solar calendar with 30- and 31-day months. Also, there was the added twist of a
130 leap year. This meant that every four years, one day was added to February to make up for the extra ¼-day each year. Because of this bright idea, Julius Caesar gave his name to a month. The month of Quintilis was changed to *July.*

135   Caesar's calendar had been the best so far, but it was still not quite right. The solar cycle is only *about* 365¼ days long. Actually, it's 11 minutes and 14 seconds short of that. Although this doesn't sound like a lot, after 400 years, the Julian calendar came out three days ahead. By
140 the 16th century, the calendar made the spring **equinox** arrive 10 days early. That just wouldn't do for planning the date for spring festivals.

Pope Gregory XIII was the man to locate the answer. What did he do? He changed the rule for leap years. He
145 made the case that for the "century" years, only the ones that could be divided evenly by 400 would be leap years.

radical

extreme; drastic

Julius Caesar

equinox

the first day of spring or fall, when day and night are equal length

The century years 1700, 1800, and 1900 were not leap years. But the year 2000 was. The year 2400 will also be.

150 The Pope made the future calendar take shape. (It became the *Gregorian calendar.*) But he still had to fix his own. What could he do? He had to drop some days. In 1582, October 4 was followed by October 15. That created a fine mess with time.

THE MAYANS

Later, the ancient Mayans used two calendars in their
155 civilization. One was a **sacred** calendar of 260 days that marked religious feasts.

The other calendar was used to keep track of time. This calendar consisted of five time periods. These were like our day, month, year, decade, and century. First,
160 there was the single day, called a *kin*. Twenty *kins* made up a month, known as a *uinal*. The Maya year of 360 days, called the *tun*, consisted of 9 *uinals*. Twenty *tuns*, or years, made the *katun*, which was 7,195 days long. Twenty *katuns*
165 composed the great period known as the *baktun*, which lasted about 143,905 days, or about 394 years.

If the Mayan people wanted to write down a certain day, they used these five periods to record
170 the number of days since time began. To do this, they gave a number to each of these periods. The number indicated how many *baktuns, katuns, tuns, uinals,* and *kins* to count since the beginning of their time calendar.

Reproduction of a Mayan calendar.

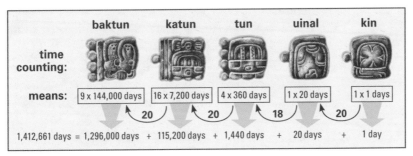

	baktun	katun	tun	uinal	kin
time counting:					
means:	9 x 144,000 days	16 x 7,200 days	4 x 360 days	1 x 20 days	1 x 1 days
		20	20	18	20
1,412,661 days =	1,296,000 days +	115,200 days +	1,440 days +	20 days +	1 day

The five periods of time on a Mayan calendar.

EUROPE AND AMERICA

At last, 170 years later, England and the American
175 colonies made the move to a revised calendar. By then,
they had 11 days to drop. Other Europeans also made the
change. Russia didn't adopt the revised calendar until 1918!
They had to skip 13 days. Another case of missing time!

Today, we've still got that same calendar. And we're
180 pretty sure what day it is. Aren't we?

Adapted from "Egypt: The Sky and the Nile" by Robert S. Bianchi,
"China: Sun, Moon, and Animals" by Karen Kane,
"Calendar Confusion" by Kelly Musselman, and
"Maya Writing and the Calendar" by David Stuart

Think About It

1. How long do the lunar and solar cycles last?

2. How did the Egyptians' system of marking time help farmers?

3. What unique associations do the Chinese use with their calendar?

4. Like the Mayans, many cultures have holidays or special days throughout the year. Describe a holiday that your family celebrates.

5. How do you think the Romans felt when holidays and seasons came at the wrong times? Describe how your life would be affected if that happened in today's world.

6. Why do you think it is important to have an accurate calendar?

THE TIME MACHINE

By H.G. Wells
Based on an adaptation by Les Martin

What is time? Is time travel possible? For centuries, these questions have **intrigued** **mystics**, **philosophers**, and scientists. Science fiction authors have had various uses for time machines, including
5 dinosaur hunting, tourism, visits to one's ancestors, and animal collecting. Ever since the time of H.G. Wells' famous novel *The Time Machine* (1895), people have grown increasingly intrigued by the idea of traveling through time. In this book, the **protagonist**
10 uses a "black and polished brass" Time Machine to gain mechanical control over time as well as to return to the present to bring back his story and assess the **consequences** of the present on the future.

In the following passage from *The Time Machine*,
15 H.G. Wells' protagonist, the Time Traveler, takes his first flight in the Time Machine he has invented.

intrigued
fascinated or interested

mystics
people who study life's mysteries

philosophers
people who study life, truth, and knowledge

protagonist
the main character

consequences
effects; results

"It was almost four in the morning, and I had finished my work, so I measured the levers one last time, and now, only one thing was left to do. I had to give the Time Machine its first test.

H.G. Wells

"I sat down in the seat of the Time Machine and looked at my pocket watch; it said nineteen minutes after four. I held my breath as I gripped the lever and pulled it down a tiny bit. How can I say what it felt like? Only that it felt like falling; it felt like falling through endless space. My stomach was trying to squeeze into my throat, and my mouth was open; it looked like the mouth of a fish—a fish gasping in air.

"Quickly, I pulled the stop lever and felt a slight bump and the machine came to a stop. I looked around and my heart sank.

"My tools were exactly where I had laid them, my coat still hung over a chair, and my workshop was just as I had left it; my machine was a failure.

"Next, I saw daylight streaming in the window, and my heart beat faster. As I looked at a clock on the mantle, the clock said half past nine; I pulled out my pocket watch and looked at it; it said twenty-one minutes after four. I had traveled through time! I had traveled more than five hours in just two minutes; my Time Machine had worked!

"At that point, I suppose I should have stopped and planned my next move, but I had waited too long for this moment. I could not wait any longer to journey through time, so I pulled down the lever again, and this time I pulled it a bit harder and farther. Time outside the machine was speeding up; I could hardly

55 believe what I was seeing. I saw my housekeeper whiz
   into the room, clean it in record time, and shoot out
   the door. It was clear that she could not see me.

   "I had to take the next step, so this time, I pulled
   the lever even farther down. The window grew dark
60 and then it brightened, then it darkened again. Time
   was speeding by; days went by like blinking lights as
   I pulled down on the lever still more. Daylight and
   darkness became a blur, and the windows and walls
   of my workshop **vanished**. The machine was swaying
65 now, and my mind was swaying, too. I decided to pull
   the lever all the way down.

   "The next thing I saw around me was a world of
   wonders. Huge buildings were rising taller and taller;
   skies were changing from dark gray to bright blue; the
70 countryside grew greener and greener. What a fantastic
   show! It was hard to turn my eyes away, and when I
   did, I looked at the dials. They told me how fast and
   far I was traveling. I was shocked; I had gone much
   faster and farther than I thought. I was in the year AD
75 802,701. Those huge numbers made me lose my head,
   and I was in a panic; I yanked hard on the stop lever.

vanished
disappeared
quickly

*The Time Machine as shown in
the 1960 Hollywood movie.*

"At last, I paid the price because the stop was too sharp and the machine tipped over. I was thrown from my seat. Stunned, I lay on soft green grass. I heard a
80 very loud thunderclap, and a shower of hailstones stung my face. It was impossible to see. "A fine welcome," I muttered, "a man travels over 800,000 years for a visit, and this is the greeting he gets!" Then the hail thinned, the sun shone through a break in the clouds, and I got
85 my first good look at the world of the future."

Think About It

1. In what year was the classic novel *The Time Machine* by H.G. Wells published?

2. When the Time Traveler first tried his Time Machine, he thought it had failed. Why did he think so? Find the place in the text that explains why he thought he had failed.

3. The next time he pulled the lever, what did the Time Traveler see that made him realize time was speeding by?

4. What do you think was happening in this passage, as described by the Time Traveler?

    The window grew dark and then it brightened, then it darkened again. Time was speeding by; days went by like blinking lights as I pulled down on the lever still more. Daylight and darkness became a blur, and the windows and walls of my workshop vanished.

5. At the end of the passage that you read, the Time Traveler says," . . . I got my first good look at the world of the future." Imagine that a person from the ancient past traveled into the present time. List at least ten things in our present time that the visitor from the past would find shocking.

6. What do you think the visitor from the past would find the same about human beings today and in his or her own time?

If you could travel into time, as some suggest we can,
You'd have to choose your when and where, the target where you'd land.

You'd ask yourself, just who would be the one you'd like to meet?
Someone who'd know about your past? Someone you'd like to greet?

5 Suppose you travel back and find Great-Grandma shoveling snow.
You'd meet, you'd introduce yourself, but Grandma wouldn't know.

She never would have met your mom, cause she had not been born;
She wouldn't know your smiling face, your jeans whose knees are torn.

So if you met, you'd have to tell her how you'd sped through time,
10 You'd see her squint and frown, and she'd suspect you'd done a crime.

She'd tell you, "Dear, I hate to say, there's just no evidence.
You traveled back and forth in time? This is just plain nonsense."

The past, perhaps, is not a place where you would be believed.
Where people would accept you; where you'd be well received.

15 Perhaps in traveling into time, a future destination
Might be the place where you could find intriguing information.

Just think! Yes, you could meet yourself three dozen years from now,
Or spin ahead three thousand years, and then, you'd take your bow.

You might be looked upon as quaint; an early human version
20 Of what the future people are—if you take that excursion.

But ask yourself, before you go, "What could I do today?"
It's only in the here and now that you can find your way.

There's everything you haven't done, but need to do in time.
You really haven't got the time to travel into time.

FRENCH

STEP 1

Phonemic Awareness and Phonics

Unit 11 introduces consonant blends and clusters.

Consonants

- **Blends** are consonant sound pairs in the same syllable. The consonants are not separated by vowels.

  Initial blends are letter combinations that represent two different consonant sounds at the beginning of a word.

  <u>l</u> blends: <u>**bl**</u>-, <u>**cl**</u>-, <u>**fl**</u>-, <u>**gl**</u>-, <u>**pl**</u>-, <u>**sl**</u>-

  <u>r</u> blends: <u>**br**</u>-, <u>**cr**</u>-, <u>**dr**</u>-, <u>**fr**</u>-, <u>**gr**</u>-, <u>**pr**</u>-, <u>**shr**</u>-, <u>**thr**</u>-, <u>**tr**</u>-

  <u>s</u> blends: <u>**sc**</u>-, <u>**sk**</u>-, <u>**sm**</u>-, <u>**sn**</u>-, <u>**sp**</u>-, <u>**st**</u>-

  <u>w</u> blends: <u>**dw**</u>-, <u>**sw**</u>-, <u>**tw**</u>-

  Final blends are letter pairs that represent two different consonant sounds at the end of a word. Final blends include: -<u>**mp**</u>, -<u>**nd**</u>, -<u>**sk**</u>, -<u>**st**</u>, -<u>**ct**</u>, -<u>**lk**</u>, -<u>**lt**</u>, -<u>**sp**</u>.

- **Clusters** consist of three or more consecutive consonants in the same syllable. Consonant clusters include: <u>**scr**</u>, <u>**spl**</u>, <u>**spr**</u>, <u>**str**</u>.

  In both blends and clusters, each consonant is pronounced.

Word Recognition and Spelling

Using Unit 11 sound-spelling correspondences, we can read and spell words like the unit words below.

Initial Blends

l blends: **bl**ock, **cl**ass, **fl**at, **gl**ad, **pl**an, **sl**ip

r blends: **br**ide, **cr**ab, **dr**op, **fr**og, **gr**ape, **pr**ize, **shr**ink, **thr**ee, **tr**ade

s blends: **sc**ale, **sk**ill, **sm**ash, **sn**ake, **sp**ot, **st**and

w blends: **dw**ell, **sw**im, **tw**in

Final Blends

ca**mp**, sa**nd**, a**sk**, la**st**

a**ct**, si**lk**, ki**lt**, gra**sp**

Clusters

scraps, **spl**ash, **spr**ing, **str**ing

Spelling Rule: Drop e

Review: The **Drop e Rule** explains what to do when adding suffixes to words with a **final silent e**.

1. If the suffix begins with a vowel, drop the **e** from the base word. Example: state + ing = stating

2. If the suffix begins with a consonant, do not drop the **e** from the base word. Example: state + ment = statement

Unit 11 Essential Words

body	every	thought
each	know	very

Spelling Lists

The Unit 11 spelling lists contain two word categories:

1. Words with initial or final blends and clusters
2. **Essential Words** (in italics)

Spelling Lists

Lessons 1–5		Lessons 6–10	
block	spot	asked	frosted
body	spring	blaming	glasses
clapping	string	brakes	golf
each	track	champs	grill
every	*thought*	crash	lunch
know	*very*	desktop	o'clock
scraps	wind	drinks	scale
splash		fresh	

Vocabulary and Morphology

Unit Vocabulary

Sound-spelling correspondences from Unit 11 and previous units make up this unit's vocabulary. Some of these words, which appeared in earlier units, are here for practice specifically with blends and clusters.

- What do these words mean?

- Do some of them mean more than one thing? Which ones?

UNIT Vocabulary

Blends and Clusters

act	drive	grass	silk	stock
ask	drop	grave	skate	stone
band	dwell	hand	skill	stop
black	else	land	smoke	stove
blaze	fact	last	snake	strap
block	fast	list	soft	swim
brave	flame	milk	solve	tense
bride	flat	past	splash	track
camp	flute	plan	split	trade
class	frame	plant	spot	trip
clock	fresh	plate	stale	wind
close	frog	prize	stand	
cost	glad	sand	state	
crime	glass	scale	stick	
cross	grape	sense	still	

Word Relationships

Word Relationships	What Is It?	Unit 11 Examples
antonyms	Words that have opposite meanings	ask/tell; open/close; fresh/rotten
synonyms	Words that have the same or similar meaning	grab/grasp; fast/quick; close/shut
homophones	Words that sound the same but have different meanings	mussed/must; know/no; close/clothes
attributes	Words that tell more about other words, such as size, parts, color, shape, texture, material, and function	a **blond** wig, the skunk's **stripe**, a **glass** plate

Meaning Parts

Review: Adding *-'s* to a singular noun signals singular possession. This means that one person or thing owns one or more things. Example: the bride's ring, the bride's rings

■ Adding **'s** can also mean that one person or thing has, or takes, something.

> **Singular Possessives**
>
> The **plane's path** means the path that is taken by the plane.
>
> One plane takes one path.

■ Adding **s'** signals plural possession. This means that more than one person or thing owns, has, or takes something.

> **Plural Possessives**
>
> The **planes' paths** means the paths that are taken by the planes.
>
> More than one plane takes a path.

STEP 4

Grammar and Usage

Verb Phrases

Review: A **verb phrase** is a group of words that:

1. Does the job of a verb

2. Conveys tense (time)

3. Has two parts: **helping verb** and **main verb**

In the sentence "The clocks will chime," *will chime* is a verb phrase. This phrase tells future time.

Future Progressive Verbs

Review: Action verbs sometimes have helping verbs. *Am, is, are, was, were,* and *will* can be used as helping verbs with action verbs.

■ The **-ing** ending on a main verb can also be used with the helping verbs **will be** to signal ongoing action in future time. This is the future progressive form of the verb.

> **Future Progressive**
> she **will be planting**; they **will be planting**

■ When we use the future progressive in speaking, we often contract the subject and **will**.

> **Future Progressive Contractions With Will**
> | I will | = | I'll | I'**ll** be going |
> | you will | = | you'll | you'**ll** be going |
> | he will | = | he'll | he'**ll** be going |

Tense Timeline

Yesterday	Today	Tomorrow
Past	Present	Future
		will be + verb + **-ing**

Unit 11 Verbs

Base Verb	Future Progressive	Base Verb	Future Progressive
act	will be acting	skate	will be skating
camp	will be camping	solve	will be solving
drive	will be driving	stand	will be standing
plant	will be planting	swim	will be swimming

Irregular Past Tense Verbs

Review: Some verbs signal past time through irregular verb forms.

Unit 11 Verbs (Irregular)

Base Verb	Irregular Past Tense	Base Verb	Irregular Past Tense
bend	bent	know	knew
bring	brought	spend	spent
drive	drove	think	thought
hit	hit		

Compound Sentences

Review: A **compound sentence** is two sentences joined by a conjunction.

Review: **Conjunctions** join words, phrases, or clauses in a sentence. Coordinating conjunctions connect words with the same function. The word **and** is a conjunction that relates similar ideas.

■ The conjunction **but** signals contrasting ideas.

> The hurricane hit land.
>
> The people escaped.
>
> The hurricane hit land, **but** the people escaped.

In this compound sentence, the base sentences *The hurricane hit land* and *The people escaped* are joined by the conjunction **but**.

The diagram below shows how to build this compound sentence with two base sentences.

Form: N/V + N/V noun/verb + noun/verb
Function: S/P + S/P subject/predicate + subject/predicate

The hurricane **hit land, but** the people escaped.

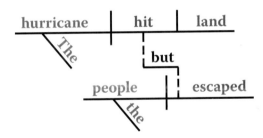

Listening and Reading Comprehension

Informational and Narrative Text

■ Some **informational** text is organized by **time sequence**. This text includes ideas, facts, evidence, or examples organized in the order in which they happened. **Transition words** signal this organization.

> **Transition Words for Time Sequence**
>
> first, next, last
>
> first, consequently, finally
>
> yesterday, today, tomorrow
>
> the first stage, the next stage, the final stage

■ **Narrative** text tells a story. When we read a story, we listen or look for the parts of a story: characters, setting, events, and resolution.

Context Clues

■ **Context clues** help us understand new vocabulary. Pronoun referents, meaning signals, and visuals, such as pictures, charts, and graphs, provide meaning links.

Signal Words

■ Some sentences ask us to remember information from what we have read or heard. Other sentences are a little harder. They ask us to read or listen, and then put information together to build meaning. These sentences ask us to **Understand It**. They use specific signal words.

> **Signal Words for Understand It**
>
> categorize, classify, discuss, match, sort

Speaking and Writing

We use different types of sentences when we speak and write.

Statements: Fact or Opinion

- Some sentences present facts or opinions. These are called **statements**.

> **Statements**
>
> **The center of a hurricane is called the eye.** This tells us a fact about a hurricane.
>
> What? The center of a hurricane is called the eye.
>
> **Everybody loves to fly kites.** This expresses an opinion about kite flying.
>
> What? Everybody loves it.

Signal Words

- Some sentences ask for information. They require putting information or ideas together to create an answer. They use specific **signal words**.

> **Signal Words for Understand It**
>
> **Categorize** the list of kites according to their use.
>
> **Classify** the kinds of storms those conditions create.
>
> **Discuss** the Chinese general's plan to use a kite.
>
> **Match** the sequence of events to the time sequence transition words.
>
> **Sort** the list of kites by use.

Paragraph Organization

- Some paragraphs are organized by **time sequence**. These paragraphs include ideas, facts, evidence, or examples organized in a sequence. **Transition words** signal this organization. Examples: first, consequently, finally

More About Words

- **Bonus Words** use the same sound-spelling correspondences from Unit 11 and previous units. Some of these words, which appeared in earlier units, are here for practice specifically with blends and clusters.

- **Idioms** are common phrases that cannot be understood by the meaning of their separate words—only by the entire phrase.

- **Word History** explains the origin of the words *wind* and *window*.

UNIT Bonus Words

bent	crate	grove	rinse	stole
blade	crude	hint	scope	strand
blame	dense	jilt	scrap	strict
bond	disk	kilt	sent	strip
brake	draft	lapse	shelve	strode
brand	drift	limp	slid	stroke
brass	drove	mast	slip	struck
broke	fist	mist	smile	strung
cast	fond	o'clock	snap	tribe
clam	froze	plot	snide	trite
click	gland	plump	span	trust
cliff	glimpse	pond	spin	twin
crab	grant	pride	spit	
crack	grasp	prose	spoke	
craft	grid	pulse	staff	
crane	grim	quilt	stake	

Idioms	
Idiom	**Meaning**
be in full swing	be at the highest level of activity
be out of your hands	be no longer within your responsibility or in your care
be out to lunch	not be in touch with the real world
be over the hump	be past the worst or most difficult part
catch red-handed	catch someone in the act of doing something wrong
go up in smoke	be totally destroyed
send someone packing	dismiss someone abruptly
hit close to home	affect your feelings or interests
snap out of it	go back to your normal condition from depression, grief, or self-pity
stack the deck	order things against someone

 **Word History**

Wind and Window—*Wind* is a very old word. *Beowulf,* a famous Old English epic poem about a brave warrior and an evil monster, contained the word *wind.* The poem was first written down in the 700s and spelled the word *wind* the same way we spell it today.

The word *window* is related to the word *wind. Window* was once spelled "windauga;" *Auga* meant "eye." The word *window* meant "wind-eye." The "wind-eye" allowed light and air to flow into the house, just like the eye let the view flow into a person's awareness.

Facts About Kites

What can fly without wings? What has a tail but not a face? What gets stuck on a branch in the comics? What can you pull but not push? You got it. It's a kite.

Think about a fine, strong wind. In one hand is a
5 stick. On the stick is lots of string. In the left hand is a kite. The string is tied to the kite's frame. Undo the string as you run. The wind lifts the kite into the air. The string slips from your hand. If there's wind, the kite is up. It's off! It takes skill. It takes wind. It takes
10 luck! The kite drifts up until it is just a speck.

Where did kites come from? What prompted the thought? It was the wind. The wind grabbed a man's hat. It was still tied to his chin. He felt the strong wind's tug. It made him think. What if I tied fabric to
15 a string? What if I held the string in my hand? The wind would make the cloth fly. He made it. From this thought, kites came about.

When was this? It was 200 BC! At this time, kites were not for fun. Kites were used to pass thoughts.
20 They helped make contact. In combat, kites sent coded facts. The facts could help one side win. Kites were used like this for a long time.

Kites: Shapes and Uses

What do you know about kites? Kites have many shapes and uses. Think about a kite. What shape is it? It could have a diamond shape. The frame is shaped like a cross. A kite could have a V shape. The frame is
5 not flat. The kite could have a box shape. The frame is four-sided. Cloth or plastic is put on the frame. This lets it catch the wind.

Kites can have long tails. Without a tail, the diamond kite spins. The tail adds mass. It stops the
10 spinning. Some kites can fly without tails. The box kite is one. Its shape lets it fly and not spin. The shape of a kite and its use are linked.

Kites have been used in combat. We know they sent coded facts. In fact, kites have had many uses. They
15 have helped us grasp things about our planet. How hot is it up in the sky? In the past, kites helped us know. One string held many kites. A strong wind lifted them up. When all of the kites landed, they had the facts.

We know who Ben Franklin is. Did you know
20 the story about how he used kites? Franklin gazed at lightning in the sky. He asked himself, "What sets it off? Can I catch it? Can I use it?" Big flashes lit up the sky. Ben sent up a kite. A key hung from the string. The lightning hit the key. This gave him ideas. In time,
25 someone would expand on what he did.

Big things have come from small kites. They were used in combat. They helped us know about our planet. They prompted us to invent things. We still use kites. We use them when the wind is strong. Get a kite.
30 Have fun!

Kites come in many shapes and sizes.

HURRICANE!

It's summer! Dangerous storms are coming. These storms are hurricanes. They are strong storms. They are twisting storms. They can be hundreds of miles wide. They take unpredictable paths. They can spin
5 toward land. These storms are feared. They threaten life. They threaten **property**.

Hurricanes begin in the late summer. They begin in tropical waters. They start in warm seas. How warm does the water have to be? The sea surface must be
10 very warm. It has to be at least 80 degrees Fahrenheit. This would be 26 degrees Centigrade.

Hurricanes are not like **ordinary** storms. They are different. They have powerful, spinning winds. The winds rotate. They whip around the storm center. The
15 center is the eye of the storm. Earth's rotation affects the direction of the spin. North of the equator, winds spin to the right. In the south, they spin to the left. This is called the *Coriolis effect*. These whirling winds

property
things or land owned by someone

ordinary
common; average quality

are dangerous. They cause a thunderstorm to form. It
20 will become a tropical storm. Then, it will become a
hurricane.

To begin, strong thunderstorms form. This happens
over open seas. This happens in warm Atlantic water
during the late summer. Warm air rises. The warm
25 air is wet. It condenses. It turns into clouds. Then, the
heat and moisture come together. The heat bursts. It
explodes. Strong thunderstorms combine. What if they
keep growing? They will become a hurricane.

Next, the thunderstorm becomes a tropical storm.
30 To do this, it needs a seed. The seed is usually a
band of low pressure. It reaches the thunderstorm.
Thunderstorms combine with high winds. They create
a thunderstorm cluster. This cluster becomes an
organized system. It has a **definite** area. Its winds are
35 strong. They blow between 39 and 73 mph. The winds
spin. A tropical storm is born.

Then the tropical storm becomes a hurricane. Two
things must be in place. They are wind strength and
wind spin. First, the sustained winds must be 74 mph
40 or higher. A sustained wind is a **continuous** wind.
Many storms have strong wind gusts. But sustained
winds are not gusting winds. They are not short winds.
Second, the winds spin. They spin around the eye.
When these two events happen, the storm has become
45 a hurricane!

Consequently, the hurricane builds strength. It
feeds on warm air. It feeds on moist air. It begins
to move. It moves between 10 and 50 mph. The

band
a narrow strip

definite
clear; easy to see;
specific

continuous
going without
stopping

en route
on the way

Spanish explorers, **en route** to the West
Indies after Columbus, encountered storms
of incredible violence. Called *huracan*, or
"evil wind," by the local people, these
storms are now known as hurricanes.

towering clouds form a wind wall. This wall holds the
50 strongest winds. It holds the heaviest rains. The wall
surrounds the eye. The strong winds spin wildly. They
whirl around the eye. Their speeds are intense! They
sometimes get up to 200 mph. If the hurricane hits
land, flooding and destruction follow.

55   Finally, the hurricane ends. The hurricane hits an
area of cool land or water. It enters a cold, unfriendly
surrounding. It loses its supply of hot, moist air. There is
nothing to feed it. The eye disappears. The storm is dead.

How are hurricanes categorized?

    The hurricane scale is numbered one to five.
60 Categories are based on wind strength. See the
chart below.

HURRICANE INTENSITY CHART

The Hurricane Scale ranks hurricanes from **Category 1** to **Category 5**.

- **Category 1 Hurricane**. Winds 74-95 mph (64-82 kt). No real damage to buildings. Damage to mobile homes. Some damage to poorly built signs. Also, some coastal flooding. Minor pier damage.

- **Category 2 Hurricane**. Winds 96-110 mph (83-95 kt). Some damage to building roofs, doors, and windows. Considerable damage to mobile homes. Flooding damages piers. Small craft in unprotected moorings may break their moorings. Some trees blown down.

- **Category 3 Hurricane**. Winds 111-130 mph (96-113 kt). Some structural damage to small residences and utility buildings. Large trees blown down. Mobile homes and poorly built signs destroyed. Flooding near the coast destroys small structures. Large structures damaged by floating debris. Land may flood far inland.

- **Category 4 Hurricane**. Winds 131-155 mph (114-135 kt). More extensive wall failure. Some complete roof structure failure on small homes. Major erosion of beach areas. Land may flood very far inland.

- **Category 5 Hurricane**. Winds 156 mph and up (135+ kt). Many complete roof failures. Some complete buildings fail. Small utility buildings blown over or away. Major flood damage to lower floors. All structures near shoreline affected. Massive evacuation of residential areas.

From the Saffir-Simpson Hurricane Scale, www.nhc.noaa.gov/HAW2/english/basics/saffir_simpson.shtml

Answer It

Say each answer in a complete sentence.

1. Categorize the kind of storm that occurs when a thunderstorm becomes an organized system.

2. Classify the kind of storm created when spinning winds top 74 mph.

3. Once a hurricane develops, describe how it finally stops.

4. Predict what kind of destruction can happen when a hurricane hits land.

5. Summarize the stages of a hurricane. (Hint: Use your time sequence transition words to help guide your answer: To begin, next, then, consequently, finally.)

A Kite's Tale

Everybody loves kites. For more than 2,000 years, people have flown kites on windy days. One tale says that the first kite was invented in China. A wind gust blew off a farmer's hat. His hat was tied on. The

5 farmer got his hat back. He also got a great idea! He couldn't have known how long his idea would live. It would fly sky high! Since then, people have made many kinds of kites. They are found all over the world. They have many **practical** uses. They've been used by the

10 military. They've been used for science experiments. They've been used to learn about flight. Today, they're just plain fun.

At first, kites were used for military purposes. The first recorded kite flight was around 200 BC. A

15 Chinese general planned to invade an enemy's palace. He would use a tunnel. First, he had to see how long to build the tunnel. How far was the palace from the wall? He decided to use the wind to find out. He would fly a kite over the wall. The flight of the kite would

20 measure the distance. For the next 1,000 years or so, kite flying remained a military activity. It was used for observation and signaling. Later, kites were used to drop information fliers.

Then, scientists began using kites. One example

25 took place in Scotland. It was a windy day in 1749. Alexander Wilson joined several kites on the same line. He lifted a thermometer into the air. He measured

practical
useful, handy

The kites dance high in the sky . . . the strings sing while they fly.

The Chinese word for kite is *fengzheng*. *Feng* means "wind." (It rhymes with *hung*.) *Zheng* means " **compete** ." (It sounds like *jung*.)

compete
to be in a contest

the air temperature. He did this again, at different
altitudes. This was the first reported scientific flight
30 of kites. Three years later, a famous kite flew. American
folklore tells of a Philadelphia flight. Benjamin
Franklin stretched his silk handkerchief between two
sticks. He sailed it during a wind-driven lightning
storm. He learned about electricity.

35   A little later, kites were used to study flight.
Engineers began to design planes. Of course, kites were
not flying machines. They couldn't stay up without
wind. Nevertheless, kite design contributed to flight. In
1893, Australian scientist Lawrence Hargrave invented
40 the box kite. Hargrave found that a box structure had
greater **stability**. It had more lifting power than kites
of old. This became the **basis** for the biplane. Many
early airplanes were biplanes. In part, they were based
on Hargrave's box kite. A few years later, the Wright
45 brothers made a five-foot kite model of a glider. They

altitudes
heights above the
Earth's surface

stability
strength and
security

basis
a starting point

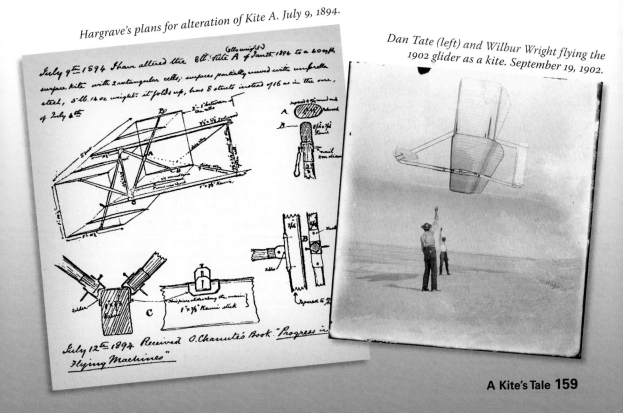

Hargrave's plans for alteration of Kite A. July 9, 1894.

Dan Tate (left) and Wilbur Wright flying the
1902 glider as a kite. September 19, 1902.

theories

views or opinions that have not yet been proven true

wanted to test flight **theories** . Again, a simple kite contributed to complex science.

Today, kites are used for fun. Thousands are sold every year. People fly kites in the park. They fly kites at
50 carnivals. Kites are seen at festivals around the world. Kites bring out the kid in everyone. Margo Brown is past president of the American Kitefliers Association. She finds kite flying relaxing. Margo says, "Putting a 'heavier-than-air' object in the air and keeping it
55 stable? It's exhilarating. It's really quite beautiful. Life is full of simple pleasures." So the next time your day is windy, go fly a kite!

Adapted from "A Kite's Tale" by Rebecca Higbee

Answer It
Say each answer in a complete sentence.

1. Discuss the Chinese general's plan to use a kite for military use. Do you think the general's plan worked? How do you know from reading the article?

2. List different ways that kites have been used. Add your own ideas to those from the article.

3. Sort the list from question 2 into categories according to how they are used.

4. Match the sequence of kite uses below to the time sequence transition words.

Transition Words:	Kite Uses:
at first	a. Scientists began using kites.
later	b. Kites were used to drop
then	information fliers.
a little later	c. Kites are used for fun.
today	d. Kites were used for military
	purposes.
	e. Kites were used to study flight.

5. Paraphrase how kites are used today.

THE DUST BOWL

THIS IS JACK OLSEN, THE VOICE OF KOKA RADIO.
YESTERDAY: SUNDAY, APRIL 14, 1935.

A wall of dust approaching a Kansas town.

The day dawned clear and dry across the southern
Great Plains. Families went to church. Some planned
5 to enjoy picnics, while others were bound for visits to
friends and family. Everyone looked forward to the
pleasant afternoon hours ahead.

Then, suddenly, in midafternoon, the air turned
cooler. Birds began fluttering nervously and all at
10 once, the wind picked up. Suddenly, a rolling black
cloud of dust darkened the northern horizon. Everyone
hurried home. We were trying desperately to beat the
overwhelming "black blizzard" before it struck. Within
minutes, the sky overhead was dark. Streetlights
15 flickered in the gloom, and drivers turned on their

Great Plains

the grassland region of central North America extending from Canada to Texas

headlights. Soon, the swirling dust storm blotted out our sun.

"Black blizzards" are nothing new to us; we residents of the southwestern plains have experienced
20 these terrible dust storms for several years now. We know their destruction. But the wall of flying soil that struck us yesterday was awesome. Its size and intensity had never been seen before.

In this morning's newspaper, one reporter writes,
25 "An uncorked jug placed on a sidewalk for two hours was half filled with dust. Lady Godiva could have ridden through the streets, and even the horse wouldn't have seen her." One neighbor said, "All we could do about it was just sit in our dusty chairs, gaze
30 at each other through the fog that filled the room, and watch that fog settle slowly and silently, covering everything—including ourselves—in a thick, brownish gray blanket."

We are getting the same reports from all over the
35 Great Plains. Our region is becoming known as the Dust Bowl. The people we know—our families and friends—are experiencing tragedy the likes of which we have never seen. We have heard stories of attics collapsing under the weight of tons of dust. Farmers'
40 tractors have been buried beneath six-foot drifts of dirt. Travelers are stranded in their cars, the roads disappearing under the dirt.

THIS IS THE VOICE OF KOKA RADIO. JACK OLSEN, SIGNING OFF.

45 JANUARY 1, 1940. THIS IS JACK OLSEN, SIGNING ON
FOR KOKA.

The new year is here. We share with the people of
our region a voice of restored hope. Our hope is for the
new decade. Those of us who have lived in the Great
50 Plains during the thirties have lived through a time
that has taken many of our homes and our lives.

During the decade of the thirties, powerful storms
of dust **ravaged** our farming and grazing lands. At
times, the winds were so powerful they cut to levels
55 as deep as a steel plow could reach. Just how bad was
it? When winds stripped the soil away, people found
long-buried Indian campgrounds, arrowheads, pioneer
wagon wheels, and even Spanish stirrups. A day rarely
passed without dust clouds rolling over. One little
60 boy in Texas said, "These storms are like rolling black
smoke. We have to keep the lights on all day. We go to
school with headlights on and with dust masks on."

But on this New Year's Day, my friends, we have
much reason for hope. Before the "dirty thirties,"
65 as our time has come to be known, our region had
experienced years of bumper crops. The years 1926,
1929, and 1931 produced particularly fine wheat crops.
Farmers were encouraged by their bountiful crops.
They began to use more efficient machinery, and they
70 carved out even greater fields. They didn't realize they
were creating a problem. What happened was this: The
farmers unknowingly uprooted the grasses that had
held together our rich prairie soil for centuries.

Then the weather changed. Less rain fell and our
75 ground dried up and crumbled. Crops withered and
died. At the same time, our ever-present prairie winds
increased in strength and duration. First, the winds
shifted the topsoil; then, they lifted it and transported
it for miles. Drought and windstorms resulted. We are
80 the people of the Great Plains. Drought was not new
to us. Windstorms were not new to us. But there was

ravaged
completely
destroyed

The Dust Bowl 163

Farmers unknowingly uprooted the grasses that had held together the rich prairie soil.

one thing that was new to us—the lack of prairie grass to hold down and protect the soil. The final blow: A grasshopper **plague** struck. It wiped out all remaining
85 vegetation and completely exposed our soil.

During the height of the windstorms, it was hard to explain our problem to people in other regions. If you weren't here like we were, you couldn't have imagined what it was like. One Texas farmer said it well: "If the
90 wind blew one way, here came the dark dust from Oklahoma. Another way, and it was the gray dust from Kansas. Still another way, the brown dust from Colorado and New Mexico. Little farms were buried, and towns were blackened."

95 Recently, I spoke to Marge Betzer, a native of North Dakota. Marge recalls that during those years "the morning sky was a pale yellow. By noon, everything had turned grayish. We covered our windows, but nothing could keep out the dust."

100 Despite the hardships we have faced over the past decade, many of us chose to stay in our homes. We remained in the Dust Bowl and hoped for rain. We tried to combat the shifting earth with improved

conservation measures. An old friend of mine, an
105 Oklahoma farmer, recently told me, "All that dust
made some of the farmers leave. We stuck it out here.
We scratched, literally scratched, to live. Despite all the
dust and the wind, we were putting in crops. . . . We
had five crop failures in five years."

110 During these Dust Bowl years, life has been a
challenge. Those of us who chose to remain have battled
constantly. We fought to keep the dust out of our homes.
We taped our windows and hung wet sheets to catch
the dust. At the dinner table, we kept our cups, glasses,
115 and plates overturned until our meals were served.
Our dentists and surgeons struggled to keep their
instruments **sterile**. Our roads and railroads were often
blocked, causing delays until overworked crews could
clear them. Many of us have lost our way in the "black
120 blizzards." Some of us perished.
The cutting dust caused "dust
pneumonia." As we know only
too well, it sometimes killed
the very young and the very
125 old.

Yet most of us kept
our sense of humor. We've
heard farmers tell the tale
that, when the drought
130 was especially bad, a man
hit on the head by a single
raindrop had to be revived
by throwing two buckets
of sand in his face. One
135 of our stores advertised,

conservation

the protection of
natural resources
such as forests,
soil, and water

sterile

completely clean
with no germs or
bacteria

*Failed crops, due to dust
and drought, caused thousands
of farming families to migrate
across the country in search
of work.*

"Great bargains in real estate. Bring your own container."
There have been hunters who claimed to have shot
prairie dogs overhead—as they tunneled through the
dusty air. One farmer said, "I hope it'll rain before the
140 kids grow up. They ain't never seen none."

Those of us who have stayed have tried to
live as normal a life as possible. In spite of our
failing crops, our ever-present dust, and our dying
landscape, we have never lost hope. Our schools
145 remained open except in the worst of the storms.
Our school basketball tournaments continued. Our
farmers planted seed, hoping the winds would stop,
hoping the rains would return. Farm wives took
whatever they could spare to Saturday markets. We
150 had faith that times would change and our beloved
land would regain its former prosperity. Caroline
Henderson, an Oklahoma farm wife, wrote in 1936:
"We **instinctively** feel that the longer we travel on a
straight road, the nearer we must be coming to a turn."

155 Finally, it seems, we've reached that turn. The
worst of our terrible drought appears to be over.
Our new soil conservation measures
have taken hold, and our crops are
returning. The ravaging winds
160 have slackened, and we see
fewer dust storms. Yes, folks,
it is our hope today that the
Dust Bowl of the 1930s is

instinctively

doing something
without thinking
about it

officially over. We wish you and yours a Happy New
165 Year, a happy new decade, a bountiful harvest, and
finally, no more dust.

THIS IS JACK OLSEN, SIGNING OFF ONE MORE TIME, ON
NEW YEAR'S DAY 1940.

Based on an article by Peter Roop. *Cobblestone*, December 1983

Think About It

1. In the fourth paragraph there is an allusion. An allusion is a brief reference to a famous historical figure. Who is referred to in the allusion? Why is this allusion a vivid choice in describing the conditions of the Dust Bowl?

2. Name at least three causes of the Dust Bowl.

3. During the years of the Dust Bowl, people died from a new illness. What was it called?

4. Jack Olsen says that people never lost their sense of humor, despite the treacherous conditions. In the text, identify one humorous story told during the Dust Bowl.

5. The Dust Bowl is based on actual history. What is unusual about the way this historical selection is written? From whose point of view is the story told?

6. Imagine a dust storm striking your neighborhood. List three problems that could be caused by excessive dust in your home.

Wind Sports

For many years, adventurers have used the wind for sport. Sailing has been popular around the world for centuries. But today's wind sports are more extreme. They are more personal. Today, athletes are directly involved
5 with the wind. Three of today's most popular wind sports are windsurfing, wingsurfing, and hang gliding.

Windsurfing

Windsurfing is a young sport. We can trace its roots back to a garage. Two Southern Californians, Jim Drake, a sailor, and Hoyle Schweitzer, a surfer, dreamed it up. They
10 wondered what would happen if they attached Jim's sail to Hoyle's surfboard. By 1968, they had combined their two sports. They had created a new sport. They called it windsurfing. How did it work? The sailor stood on the board and held on to the sail.

15   Quickly, windsurfing's popularity exploded. Through the 1970s and into the 1980s, racing participation reached an all-time high. A professional World Cup tour began. By 1984, the sport was included in the Olympic Games. Today, windsurfing has become a popular wind sport all 20 over the world.

There are many types of windsurfing. They include cruising, freestyle sailing, high-wind sailing, slalom sailing, bump-and-jump sailing, and wave sailing.

Cruising

The first type of windsurfing is cruising. Cruising 25 is the most popular form of windsurfing. It is also the simplest form. What is it? Cruising is setting out for a simple sail across a lake. Cruising is going for an all-day, island-hopping sail. Cruising from point to point is one of windsurfing's most satisfying experiences.

Freestyle

30   The second type of windsurfing is called freestyle. Freestyle is almost the opposite of cruising. Freestyle sailing means putting the board and sail through a series of tricks and fancy moves. These can include turns, rail rides (riding while standing on the board's thin edge), 35 and sail spins. Some athletes make freestyle sailing their career. What they can get a board to do is remarkable. Freestyle sailing is always a crowd pleaser. Sailors from beginners to experts can enjoy freestyle sailing.

High-wind sailing

The next type is high-wind sailing. Just as it sounds, 40 high-wind windsurfing requires high winds—winds over 10 knots.* Most high-wind sailors sail in wind speeds of 15–25 knots. At this wind strength, advanced sailors get their boards onto a plane. When this happens, the board

* 1 knot is approximately 1.15 mph

maneuverable

can be moved easily

agility

the ability to move quickly and skillfully

45 skims across the surface of the water. The lift created from the board's speed lets sailors use smaller, more **maneuverable** boards. Smaller boards require the sailor to have more **agility** and quicker reflexes. They go faster. This style is not for beginners.

Slalom sailing

50   Slalom is another popular form of high-wind sailing. Sailors wait until the wind is really up. Everywhere, they're on their slalom boards, zipping back and forth. Speeds get up to 35 knots. The most excitement is in carving high-speed turns between exhilarating runs.
55 Speed makes slalom sailing one of the most exciting of all sports.

Bump-and-jump sailing

     Another type of windsurfing is bump-and-jump sailing. This style requires good winds and choppy waters. It's done in winds of 20–40 knots. Advanced sailors take
60 out their small boards. They use the waves as ramps for big jumps! On a good bump-and-jump day, jumps, turns, loops, and crashes light up the water. What is bump-and-jump sailing like? It's like slalom sailing on adrenaline.

Wave sailing

     Finally, there is wave sailing. It may be the most
65 spectacular form of windsurfing. It's certainly the most athletic. It may be the most difficult form of windsurfing. Any ocean or gulf can sometimes have wave sailing conditions. The best conditions are
70 when waves are breaking parallel to the beach. The wind must blow along the beach. Sailors use the wind to surf and jump the waves.

Talkin' like a windsurfer

75　　Windsurfers have a special language. Their language includes words like *nukin'*, *shreddin'*, and *screamin'*. These terms describe the wind's **velocity**. What do you think these terms mean? Investigate, and find a source that provides the meanings of these three windsurfing terms.

velocity
speed

Wingsurfing

80　　Wingsurfing had its beginnings on ice. In the 1990s, Scandinavians attached sails to ice surfboards and used them to slide across the ice. What exactly do today's wingsurfers do? They have invented new sports using
85　sails and the wind. When extreme sports started to become popular, young snowboarders and extreme skiers experimented. While attached to a pair of skis, a snowboard, a pair of in-line skates, or a skateboard, wing sailors held onto an ultralight wing. They changed the
90　sail design that windsurfers used. They discovered that the sail, held flat over their heads, made incredible jumps and tricks possible. Actually, this wing was better for skiing or skating than it was for windsurfing. Why? On skis or skates, the rider
95　acted as the mast. The wind provided the power. In-line skaters, skateboarders, snowboarders, and extreme skiers held sails, glided fast, and jumped high. For many extreme athletes, wingsurfing has become an addictive sport.

Hang gliding

100　　One of the oldest and most **poignant** dreams of humans has been to fly like a bird. Commercial air travel is a common experience today. But the dream of a personal, birdlike flight has **eluded** all but a very few. The adventurous men and women who fly hang gliders
105　know this experience.
　　Some think hang gliding is new to aviation. Actually, hang gliding is one of the oldest forms of

poignant
strongly felt; stimulating

eluded
stayed away from or escaped

human flight. Before the airplane, some had discovered how to copy the flights of birds. The athlete ran down a
110 hill with a light glider. He took off into the air and glided down. Interest in birdlike flight with gliders **waned**, however, after the Wright brothers invented the airplane.

waned
decreased slowly

Hang gliding owes its rebirth to a man named Rogallo, a NASA scientist. He had developed a landing
115 system for the Apollo astronauts' return to Earth. In the 1960s, he invented a new device. It included a simple, kite-like wing. The wing was made from fabric and aluminum tubing. The Rogallo wing had interesting features: simplicity of design, ease of construction, capability of
120 slow flight, and gentle landing characteristics. The wing led to an explosive growth in hang gliding. Hang gliding became a popular wind sport. For the first time in history, simple, unencumbered, birdlike flight was possible for anyone who wanted to try it.

125 Hang gliding began as simply gliding down small hills on low performance kites. Over the last three decades, it has evolved. This evolution made for new and extreme wind adventures. Today, hang gliders gain thousands of feet of altitude in updrafts (rising air currents). They fly
130 cross-country over hundreds of miles. They soar with hawks and eagles. They fly!

Think About It

1. Explain how today's wind sports are different from traditional sailing.

2. Describe the five types of windsurfing.

3. Where and when did wingsurfing originate?

4. Why do you think people have dreamed of flying like a bird? What do you think this experience would be like?

5. If you could become an expert in a wind sport, which would you choose? Why?

6. Invent a new sport by combining two separate sports. Describe your sport. Give it a name.

Grab a Sandwich

STEP 1

Phonemic Awareness and Phonics

Unit 12 reviews the sounds of English learned so far. They include consonants and vowels.

Consonants

Review: **Consonants** are closed sounds. They restrict or close the airflow using the lips, teeth, or tongue. Sometimes consonants are used in combinations:

Digraphs: Two consonants that represent one sound (**ch**, **sh**, **th**, **wh**, **-ng**)

Trigraphs: Three consonants that represent one sound (**-tch**)

Blends: Two consonants that represent two sounds (**cl-**, **br-**, **sc-**, **tw-**, **-lk**, **-mp**, **-nd**)

Clusters: Three consonants that represent three sounds (**scr-**, **spl-**, **spr-**, **str-**)

Vowels

Review: **Vowels** are open sounds. They keep the airflow open.

Short vowels: / $\breve{a}$ / as in cat; / $\breve{e}$ / as in pet; / $\breve{i}$ / as in sit; / $\breve{o}$ / as in fox; / $\breve{u}$ / as in cup

Long vowels: The long vowel sound for **a**, **e**, **i,** and **o** is the same as the name of the letter that represents it. The long vowel sound for **u** can be pronounced in two ways: / $\overline{oo}$ / as in tube, and / $y\overline{oo}$ / as in cute.

Final silent e: One pattern for long vowels is the **final silent e** as in make. The letter **e** at the end of a syllable signals a long vowel sound. The **e** is silent.

Word Recognition and Spelling

Review: We put two words together to make compound words. We put syllables together to make two-syllable words.

Compound Words

Review: **Compound words** are words made up of two or more smaller words. Example: drum + stick = drumstick

Unit 12 Compound Words

anything	jackpot	something
cutback	outside	upon
himself	someone	within

Two-Syllable Words

These Unit 12 two-syllable words have the VC/CV pattern.

VC/CV

chipmunk	disrupt	insect	publish
context	ethnic	public	suffix

These Unit 12 two-syllable words have the VC/V pattern.

VC/V

credit	ethic	polish
edit	exit	products

Contractions

Review: **Contractions** are two words combined into one word. Some letters are left out and replaced by an apostrophe (').

Contractions		
did not	=	didn't
we will	=	we'll
they would	=	they'd

Abbreviations

■ An **abbreviation** is a shortened form of a word.

Abbreviations		
Dr.	=	doctor
Oct.	=	October
CA	=	California (postal abbreviation)
DMV	=	Department of Motor Vehicles

Unit 12 Essential Words

Dr.	Mrs.	find
Mr.	Ms.	only

Note: All other Book B **Essential Words** are in the Essential Words review on page 187.

Spelling Rules

Review: The **Doubling Rule**: When adding suffixes to words that fit the **1-1-1 Rule** (one syllable, one vowel, one consonant at the end):

- Double the final consonant *before* adding a suffix that begins with a vowel. Example: shop + ing = shopping

- Do not double the final consonant when the suffix begins with a consonant. Example: cup + ful = cupful

Review: The **Drop e Rule**: When adding suffixes to **final silent e** words:

- If the suffix begins with a *vowel*, drop the **e** from the base word. Example: state + ing = stating

- If the suffix begins with a *consonant*, do not drop the **e** from the base word. Example: state + ment = statement

Spelling Lists

The Unit 12 spelling lists contain words from all previous units. There are three word categories:

1. **Essential Words** including abbreviations (in italics)

2. Contractions with **not**, **will**, **would**

3. Words with endings: **-s**, **-es**, **-ing**, **-ed**

Spelling Lists

Lessons 1–5		Lessons 6–10	
any	*Ms.*	branches	outside
been	*only*	didn't	ranch
could	passes	finished	sandwich
Dr.	running	jumped	sometimes
find	some	lifted	subtract
insects	*their*	months	they'd
Mr.	wings	outcome	we'll
Mrs.		outlast	

STEP 3

Vocabulary and Morphology

Unit Vocabulary

Words from Unit 12 and previous units make up this unit's vocabulary.

- What do these words mean?
- Do some of them mean more than one thing? Which ones?

UNIT Vocabulary

bank	from	mane	ranch	take
bones	game	match	ride	tell
branches	gave	mile	rope	than
but	get	misspell	run	themselves
came	grade	months	sale	thrive
catch	himself	much	same	thrust
close	home	name	sandwich	time
come	hope	neck	scale	trespass
credit	hunting	net	ship	until
crops	inches	note	shop	up
eggs	insects	nothing	side	upon
exam	jumped	one	size	use
expect	killed	passed	smiled	waves
express	king	pet	some	white
file	lake	picked	someone	wife
filled	late	plane	something	wings
fine	legs	printed	state	within
finished	life	products	stretched	withstand
fish	lifted	pulled	subtract	
five	long	pushed	suffix	

Expressions Review

- Idioms are common phrases that cannot be understood by the meanings of their separate words—only by the entire phrase. Example: have a bone to pick (have grounds for a complaint or dispute)

- Expressions are a common way of saying something in English. Example: off the bat (right away)

Word Relationships Review

Words are related in different ways. This chart reviews word relationships.

Word Relationships	What Is It?	Unit 12 Examples
antonyms	Words that have opposite meanings	to/from; up/down; one/many; come/go; in/out
synonyms	Words that have the same or a similar meaning	same/alike; within/inside; pull/drag; plus/add
homophones	Words that sound the same but have different meanings	one/won; some/sum; passed/past
attributes	Words that tell more about other words, such as size, parts, color, shape, function, texture, or material	plane/wing; clock/time; pillow/soft; water/wet; tree/living

Meaning Parts

Review: Adding suffixes extends words' meanings.

-s or -es	**Plural** means more than one. Adding **-s** or **-es** to a noun changes the word to mean more than one. Examples: bones, ranches
-'s or -s'	**Possession** means ownership. Adding -'s or -s' to a noun signals singular ('s) or plural (s') possessive. Examples: egg's, eggs'
-s, -ed, -ing	**Verb tense** indicates time. Adding **-s**, **-ed**, or **-ing** to a verb signals its tense or ongoing action. Examples: lifts, lifted, was lifting

Grammar and Usage

Noun Function	Explanation	Unit 12 Examples
Subject	Nouns can be the subject (S) of a sentence. The subject names the person, place, thing, or idea that the sentence is about.	S The **sandwich** got its name from the Earl of Sandwich.
Direct Object	Nouns can be the direct object (DO) of the sentence. The direct object is the person, place, or thing that receives the action.	DO People eat **sandwiches** for lunch.
Object of a Preposition	Nouns can be the object of a preposition (OP) in a sentence.	Some people put pickles PREP OP on their **sandwiches**.

Tense Timeline

Review: Verbs describe an action or a state of being. Verbs also convey time. The **Tense Timeline** shows the verb forms learned so far.

Yesterday	Today	Tomorrow
Past	Present	Future
-ed	**-s**	will + verb
was/were + verb + **-ing**	am/is/are + verb + **-ing**	will be + verb + **-ing**

Verb Tenses

Unit 12 Verbs (Regular)

Base Verb	Past Tense	Present Tense	Future Tense
bug	bugged	bug/bugs	will bug
fish	fished	fish/fishes	will fish
hope	hoped	hope/hopes	will hope
pull	pulled	pull/pulls	will pull

Some verbs have irregular past tense forms. Review the present and past forms for these Unit 12 verbs.

Unit 12 Verbs (Irregular)

Base Verb	Irregular Past Tense
forget	forgot
lend	lent
thrust	thrust
withstand	withstood

Review: **Conjunctions** join words, phrases, or clauses in a sentence. They also join sentences. Coordinating conjunctions include: **and**, **but**.

Sentence Patterns

Review: All parts of a sentence can be compounded. The compound parts are joined by a coordinating conjunction:

Subjects: *Salami **and** cheese* make a good sandwich.

Predicates: People from around the world *make **and** eat* sandwiches for lunch.

Direct objects: Some people put *tomatoes **and** pickles* on their sandwiches.

Sentences: The students made sandwiches for lunch, **but** they left them on the bus.

Listening and Reading Comprehension

Informational and Narrative Text

- Some **informational** text is organized by **time sequence**. Ideas, facts, evidence, or examples are organized according to the order in which they happened. **Transition words** signal the time sequence.

> **Transition Words for Time Sequence**
>
> first, next, last
>
> in the beginning, then, later, finally
>
> yesterday, today, tomorrow
>
> the first stage, the next stage, the final stage

- **Narrative** text tells a story. When we read a story, we listen or look for the parts of a story: characters, setting, events, and resolution.

Context Clues

- **Context clues** help us understand new vocabulary. Pronoun referents, meaning signals, and visuals, such as pictures, charts, and graphs, provide meaning links.

Signal Words

- Some sentences ask us to remember information we have read or heard. **Remember It** uses specific **signal words**. Examples: describe, list. Other sentences ask us to read or listen, and then put facts together to build meaning. These sentences ask us to **Understand It**. They use specific **signal words**.

> **Signal Words for Understand It**
>
> explain, compare, contrast

STEP 6 — Speaking and Writing

We use different types of sentences when we speak and write.

Statements: Fact or Opinion

- Some sentences present facts or opinions. These are called **statements**.

> **Statements**
>
> **The Earl of Sandwich gave sandwiches their name.**
> This tells us a fact about the word *sandwich*.
>
> What? The word comes from a person whose name was Sandwich.
>
> **A po'boy is the favorite sandwich in New Orleans.**
> This expresses an opinion about po'boys.
>
> What? The writer thinks that this is New Orleans' favorite sandwich.

Signal Words

- Some sentences ask for information. They require putting information or ideas together to create an answer. They use specific **signal words**.

> **Signal Words for Understand It**
>
> **Explain** how to make a hero sandwich.
>
> **Compare** a hero sandwich to a hamburger.
>
> **Contrast** a hero sandwich made by someone in Italy with one made by someone in New Orleans.

Paragraph Organization

- Some paragraphs are organized by **time sequence**. These paragraphs include ideas, facts, evidence, or examples organized in a sequence. **Transition words** signal this organization. Examples: the first stage, the next stage, the final stage

More About Words

- **Bonus Words** use the same sound-spelling correspondences that we have studied in this unit and previous units.

- **Idioms** are common phrases that cannot be understood by the meanings of their separate words—only by the entire phrase.

- **Word History** tells about the origin of *brief, breve,* and *abbreviate.*

- **Review Words** include Essential Words, compound words, and contractions from Units 7–11.

UNIT Bonus Words

annex	discuss	handspring	rustic
backhand	disgust	liftoff	sendoff
backstretch	disrupt	metric	shamrock
checkup	dove	offset	spendthrift
chipmunk	edit	offspring	standoff
club	ethnic	polish	thankless
context	exist	products	welcome
cutback	exit	public	whiplash
desktop	fullback	publish	zone

Idioms	
Idiom	**Meaning**
be all wet	be entirely mistaken
be out of line	be uncalled for; improper; out of control
call your bluff	challenge another with a display of strength or confidence
call the shots	exercise authority; be in charge
come to life	become excited
get on the stick	begin to work
go to bat for	give help to; defend
have a bone to pick	have grounds for a complaint or dispute
let the cat out of the bag	let a secret be known
pull a fast one	play a trick

 **Word History**

Brief, breve, and abbreviate—All three words have the same origin. An old Latin word, *brevis*, meant *short*. Today, *brief* means something that is short in length or time. A *breve* is the half-circle mark used above a vowel letter to signal a short vowel sound. To *abbreviate* is to make something shorter. An abbreviation is a shortened from of a word, such as Dr. for doctor or St. for street. What abbreviations are in this unit?

Review Words

Essential Words

about	any	know	too
all	been	many	two
almost	body	our	very
alone	call	out	word
already	could	should	would
also	each	small	write
although	every	their	
always	into	thought	

Compound Words

anybody	forget	outdoes	someone
anyhow	handout	outdone	something
anyone	letdown	outfit	somewhat
anything	outbid	outlast	somewhere
anytime	outcast	outlet	twosome
anyway	outcome	outside	without
anywhere	outdid	shutout	yourself
dugout	outdo	somehow	

Contractions

aren't	doesn't	she'd	wasn't
can't	don't	they'd	we'll
didn't	isn't	they'll	weren't

What's for Lunch?

Most of us take time for lunch. What do you like
to eat? Many of us like sandwiches. Sandwiches and
chips make a quick lunch. Some lunch times are not
very long. Some of us have to eat lunch on the run. A
5   sandwich is a snap to eat. It's quick and not messy.

Inventing the Sandwich

How did the sandwich get its name? It came from a man. His name was Sandwich. He invented it! Sandwich loved games. In the games, he used his hands. His hands could not be messy. Thinking of this,
10 he made a sandwich. It was quick to eat. It kept his hands from getting messy. It fit the bill! He could use one hand to eat. This left one hand for the game.

Making a Sandwich

Ask for a sandwich. What name did you use? Sandwiches have many names. Sandwiches come in
15 many shapes and sizes. You can have a club sandwich. You can have a sub sandwich as well. Do you like ham and swiss on a bun? Make a sandwich. A club. A sub. Make it thick. Make it thin. Just put the things you like on it. This makes quite an inviting sandwich!

A Picnic Lunch

20 Packing a lunch for a picnic? Take some sandwiches. Pack chips and drinks. Put them in a basket. Bring a blanket as well. Strap the blanket and the basket to the back of a bike. Take a long ride to a lake. You can rest when the trek is finished. Sit
25 on the blanket and kick back. Then, unpack the basket. It's time for lunch.

Making HERO Sandwiches

Hero Sandwich History

What kind of sandwiches do you like? What do you call a sandwich on French bread? What if it's stuffed with **cold cuts**? Do you live in New England? It's a grinder. Do you live on the West Coast? It's a sub. Do
5 you live in Philadelphia? It's a hoagie. Do you live in New Orleans? It's a po' boy. If you live in New York, it's called a hero. Food experts agree. The **modern** sub and hero sandwiches are all related. They're regional variations of the same sandwich.

cold cuts
cold slices of meats

modern
related to today's life; current

10   People from southern Italy introduced this kind of
sandwich. It was filled with salami, cheese, peppers,
olives, and oil. What was the grandfather of the sub?
It was probably the muffuletta. People in New Orleans
still love this **traditional** sandwich. Round Sicilian
15   bread is toasted. It is filled with fresh salami, cheese,
olive salad, and olive oil. After World War II, Italian
food became popular around the world.

       Over time, these sandwiches began to vary. People
tried different meats. They tried turkey and roast beef.
20   They used different cheeses. They tried jack, cheddar,
American, and Swiss. They added vegetables. They
tried lettuce and tomato. They added spreads like
mayonnaise and mustard.

       As time passed, this sandwich got different names.
25   Where did the hero sandwich get its name? Some
say it was named for a heroic **feat** . What feat was
that? Eating such a huge sandwich! How did the po'
boy get its name? Some say its name referred to its
cheap price. Others say it came from the French word
30   *pourboire* (pur-'bwär), which means "a tip or gratuity."
How did the sub get its name? During World War II,

traditional
relating to beliefs
or customs kept
over time

feat
an unusual skill or
ability

hundreds of hero sandwiches were ordered in one day. Who ordered hundreds of sandwiches? Workers on a submarine base placed the order.

How to Make a Hero Sandwich

35   These meat, cheese, and vegetable sandwiches are popular. They're made on Italian or French bread. Who decides what goes on your sandwich? You do! Local food tradition might sway you. Ethnic **preference** may also affect your recipe. Wherever you live, here's a basic recipe.

40   First, hold a loaf of French bread on its side. Second, slice the bread in half lengthwise. Next, layer on slices of meat and cheese. Ham and salami can be used. Provolone, Swiss, or American cheese can be used. Then, top with lettuce and tomato. After
45 that, add onions, pickles, olives, and hot peppers. Hot peppers and onions are **optional**. Finally, spread on mayonnaise or mustard. Other condiments can be added, too. A drizzle of Italian salad dressing adds a little spice. At last, be a hero. Eat that sandwich!

preference
a choice;
a selection

optional
not required; left to
one's choice

Answer It
Say each answer in a complete sentence.

1. After reading this article, explain what ingredients you would use to make a hero sandwich.

2. Draw a Venn diagram to compare and contrast the ingredients of a hero sandwich made by someone in Italy with those of a hero sandwich made by someone in New Orleans.

3. Describe how the sub sandwich got its name.

4. List three different names used for hero sandwiches. Choose a new name for these sandwiches. Explain why you chose that name and list the ingredients you would put on it. Maybe you'll begin a new trend!

5. Explain how to make a hero sandwich to a partner.

EPONYMOUS Sandwiches

Where do English words get their start? English has hundreds of thousands of words. Some words come from people's names. Others come from places. Sometimes, the name of a person or a place becomes

5 an ordinary, everyday word. We call that word an *eponym*. Years pass. More people start using the word. We use it in conversation. We use it in writing. We forget about the person. We forget about the place. But we keep using words that came from their names!

10 You eat eponymous foods every day. Don't be **suspicious**. It's true! Many common food names come from people or places. The next time you eat a sandwich, think about it. Are you eating eponymous food? Yes! How do you know? The word *sandwich* is an eponym!

> **suspicious**
> having doubt

Sandwich

15 The **Earl** of Sandwich loved to play cards. Sometimes he played cards all day. He might play all night. He didn't like to leave the game, not even

20 to eat! One morning in 1762, the earl was playing cards. He ordered his servant to bring him roast beef. He said to wrap it in bread. That way, he

> **earl**
> a British position of high social class

John Montagu,
4th Earl of Sandwich
by Joseph Highmore.

25 could hold his food in one hand. The bread would keep his fingers clean, and he could keep one hand free. He could still hold his cards and eat. That's how he invented the sandwich!

People have eaten bread for at least 6,000 years.
30 People had probably eaten sandwiches before. Nobody knows for sure. But one thing is **certain** . Once they were given his famous name, sandwiches became one of the most popular foods eaten anywhere. One estimate says that Americans alone eat 300 million
35 sandwiches every day!

certain
sure to happen

Pickles

How did people preserve food long ago? They had no refrigerators. They pickled food. This kept it from spoiling. Sometimes, food was preserved in salt water. Sometimes, people used vinegar. Who invented
40 this method? No one knows for sure. But one person who gets the credit is a Dutchman named Willem Beukelz (pronounced boi'kĕlz). In the 1300s, he pickled some food. The English liked Beukelz's idea. But they mispronounced his name! When they tried to say
45 "Beukelz," it sounded like pickles. You guessed it! That's why we call pickled cucumbers "pickles." Have a pickle with your sandwich? Have a double eponymous meal!

Cheddar

Cheddar is a hard, smooth cheese. It can be white or yellow. It can be **mild** or **sharp** . People all over the
50 world love cheddar cheese. It's so popular that lots of sandwiches come with cheddar. The first time anybody ever ate cheddar cheese was in the English village of Cheddar. That's the place where cheddar was first made. That's where cheddar got its name.

mild
not strong tasting

sharp
strong in odor or taste

Bologna

55 Bologna is a beautiful city in northern Italy. It was famous for its smoked sausages. They were made from

different meats. People all over the world
started eating Bologna sausage. Everybody
loved it. People started calling the meat
60 "bologna." Today, some people say and spell
it "baloney."

Frankfurters and Hamburgers

What are the most famous eponymous
sandwiches of all? Frankfurters and
hamburgers. Frankfurters (also called
65 hot dogs) are everywhere. They're in the
school cafeteria. They're sold at ball games.
Street stands sell frankfurters. How did they
get their name? They came from Frankfurt,
Germany.

70 Hamburgers may be even more popular.
Americans eat millions of hamburgers on
toasted buns every day. Usually, we add pickles.
We add ketchup and other condiments. Where
did these popular meat patties originate? They
75 were first made in Hamburg, Germany.

Do you know anybody who always knows
everything about everything? The next time you
want to **impress** that person, ask this question:
"What eponymous foods have you eaten
80 recently?" Then, sit back and smile.

impress
to please others

Answer It
Say each answer in a complete sentence.

1. Define *eponym* in your own words.

2. Explain how the sandwich got its name.

3. Identify the way cheddar, bologna, frankfurter, and hamburger got their names.

4. Explain how your answer to question 3 contrasts from the way sandwiches and pickles got their names.

5. Paraphrase how cheddar got its name.

Sandwiches
+
Hero
=
SUCCESS

chef
a person who prepares food; a cook

flourishing
succeeding, prospering

culinary
of or relating to cooking

Beverly Velasquez had always wanted to be a **chef**. By the time she was twelve, she was bagging chocolate chip cookies for her community center in her native Indianapolis. Today, she owns a **flourishing** sandwich
5 shop, Mo Bev's, in her old neighborhood. Focusing on healthy food, Bev and her sandwiches have brought success back to the neighborhood.

Bev studied environmental sciences at San Diego State University. Meanwhile, she worked with seafood
10 wholesalers on the dock. She moved up the ranks in a popular San Diego seafood restaurant. By 1984, she had finished **culinary** school. She did a residency with Montana National Parks. Her
15 assignment was the Many Glacier Hotel. By then, it was already clear that Bev was one fantastic chef.

Bev wasn't just good. She was great! She competed in North
20 America's Junior Culinary

Beverly Velasquez with one of her gourmet sandwiches.

Olympics. She finished second. Since then, Bev's been first in just about everything she's done. She's never stopped learning. And she's never stopped trying.

25 Her husband, David, is a native of Puerto Rico. A communications analyst in the military, he was sent to Belgium. There, Bev gained experience in European culinary traditions. She learned about Belgian delicacies and other types of foods. She had the opportunity to work with military chefs. She was chef

30 at a NATO officer's club. Soon, Bev began **catering** from her home. When they entertained, Americans stationed overseas chose Bev as their caterer.

Bev, David, and their two children lived in Belgium, Turkey, Germany, and North Carolina while David

35 was in the military. In 2000, they moved back to Indianapolis. After years of being away, Bev returned to her old neighborhood. She opened Mo Bev's.

Beverly Velasquez could have gone anywhere and become a successful chef. But instead of choosing

40 an upscale location for her business, Bev went back home. She opened her sandwich shop in her old neighborhood. Years before, the place had **bustled** with energy. But over time, the neighborhood suffered, and

45 people moved out. Businesses closed.

Bev and a group of African American business owners moved back in. They wanted to return their community to its people. Others

50 joined them. Dorothy Davis **revived** an abandoned filling station. She decorated her business, *Smart Starts Here*, with colorful murals. They

catering
preparing and providing food for banquets and parties

bustled
swarmed, buzzed

revived
brought back into use

Dorothy Davis decorated her business with colorful murals.

include figures from African American history. Walls
55 feature low pegs holding up tiny coats. Dorothy's
customers are three to five years old.

   To Mrs. Davis, Beverly Velasquez is a hero. "And
then when Mo Bev's came. . . . You have to give credit
where it's due. . . . These were just ordinary women
60 doing an extraordinary thing," she said. "Mo Bev's has
really gotten the neighborhood together. Everyone is
excited."

   Can sandwiches create heroes? Can sandwiches
breed success? If you're in Indy, just ask the people in
65 the neighborhood.

Think About It

1. Explain how Beverly Velasquez brought success back
   to her neighborhood.

2. Describe how Beverly attained her goal of becoming
   a great chef.

3. Summarize how Beverly gained experience as a chef
   while living in Europe.

4. Explain why Beverly decided to open a sandwich
   shop in her old neighborhood.

5. Dorothy Davis owns a business called *Smart Starts
   Here*, and her customers are three to five years old.
   What type of business can you infer that Dorothy
   owns? Explain.

6. Compare how Beverly Velasquez and Dorothy Davis
   could both be considered heroes.

A WORLD OF SANDWICHES

Ancient Egyptian Sandwiches

Were ancient Egyptians eating sandwiches 4,000 years ago? Clues in the ruins of tombs and old houses help answer this question.

The world's first beekeepers were Egyptians.
5 They kept hives in large pottery jars. Fearless beekeepers simply brushed the bees aside to collect their honeycombs. The honey was stored in covered containers. Family members must have enjoyed dipping their fingers in these bowls for a sweet treat. Perhaps
10 they put honey on their bread, too.

In ancient Egypt, people ate bread at every meal. In fact, bread was ancient Egypt's main food. There were hundreds of kinds of bread. It came in many different shapes and sizes. Some recipes used fruits, garlic, or
15 nuts to flavor the bread loaves.

Eating bread caused some problems, though. Bits of desert sand and stones got into the dough. Scientists have discovered that most Egyptian mummies have

worn and missing teeth. They believe that the
20 Egyptians wore their teeth down while chewing on
their bread.

So, what might ancient Egyptian people have
put into their sandwiches? It's a simple recipe. You
probably don't want to try it, though. They probably
25 cut thick slabs of bread and spread garlic on top.
Next, they piled on raw onions. Maybe that's why they
chewed mint leaves—to sweeten their breath!

Chinese Sandwiches

Throughout China, meals traditionally have two
basic parts. The first part is usually *fan* (rice) or *mian*
30 (noodles or bread). In Beijing, in the northern part
of China, farmers grow more wheat than rice. The
people make noodles, breads, and buns from wheat and
various cereals.

The second part of the Chinese meal is called *cai*.
35 These are meat, fish, and vegetable dishes. They are
served on top of noodles or inside bread. In all of these
dishes, Chinese cooks **excel** at mixing flavors, like
sweet and sour. They also mix textures, like smooth
and crispy. Beijing **reveres** many old recipes. Some
40 have been served for centuries. One duck dish, Peking
duck, has long been a favorite entrée. (*Peking* is the
English name for Beijing.) In this dish, small slices of
duck meat are wrapped into thin pancakes and eaten
like sandwiches.

45 Another Chinese "sandwich" is a popular item on
most *dim sum* menus. What's dim sum? The literal
meaning is "to touch your heart." They are little
appetizers, a variety of tasty treats. They include
dumplings, steamed dishes, and other goodies like
50 steamed buns filled with roast pork, *char siu bao*.
These may be the most fabulous sandwiches you've
ever eaten!

various
different kinds

excel
to do much better
than average

reveres
feels that
something is very
special; cherishes

Middle Eastern Sandwiches

Pocket sandwiches are a popular alternative to sandwiches made with bread. The pocket, or pita bread, comes from the Middle East. Other sandwich-like foods from the Middle East include *fattoush* and *falafel*. Fattoush combines tossed greens and tomatoes on toasted flatbread. The falafel is the original "veggie burger." It is made with fava beans, chickpeas, vegetables, and spices. Some versions also use lentils.

Bagels

The "father of the bagel" was an unknown Viennese baker. He wanted to pay tribute to the king of Poland. In 1683, King Jan had just saved the Austrian people from an onslaught of Turkish invaders. The king was an **avid** and accomplished horseman. The baker decided to shape the yeast dough into an uneven circle resembling a stirrup.

Most people accept this story as true for two reasons. First, a traditional hand-rolled bagel is never perfect in shape. It's not round, like a doughnut. A good bagel skews into a stirrup-like shape. Second, and maybe more importantly, the Austrian word for stirrup is *beugel*. No one knows who first slathered bagels with cream cheese. Actually, cream cheese was developed by English Quakers in the mid-1700s. So King Jan never tasted a bagel with cream cheese! Today, many people make sandwiches with bagels instead of bread.

Quesadillas

The origin of quesadillas can't be traced to a particular year or person. They evolved because the **ingredients** were readily available, and they were easy to make. The history of quesadillas really begins with the story of corn and the cooking of tortillas.

What do the experts tell us about tortillas? Tortillas are round and thin. They are made of corn. Corn was

avid
eager; enthusiastic

ingredients
food items used in a recipe

85 a basic food in Mesoamerica. It is not known how long tortillas have been a **staple**. When the conquistadores arrived in the New World in the late 15th century, they discovered that the inhabitants ate flat corn breads. The Spanish gave tortillas their name. Today, tortillas

90 are made of flour as well as corn. Fresh tortillas are eaten as bread, used as plate and spoon, and filled with a variety of foods. A quesadilla is made by folding a fresh tortilla in half around a simple filling such as cheese. So, what's a quesadilla? It's a sandwich!

staple

a common, basic food

Think About It

1. Why did ancient Egyptians have dental problems when they ate sandwiches?

2. What are the two parts of traditional Chinese meals?

3. If you wanted a "veggie burger" in the Middle East, what could you order? What could you expect to find in it?

4. How did the Viennese baker feel about King Jan?

5. Summarize the five types of sandwiches described in the text.

6. If you could make the perfect sandwich, how would you make it?

English Consonant Chart

(Note the voiceless/voiced consonant phoneme pairs)

Mouth Position

	Bilabial (lips)	Labiodental (lips/teeth)	Dental (tongue between teeth)	Alveolar (tongue behind teeth)	Palatal (roof of mouth)	Velar (back of mouth)	Glottal (throat)
Stops	/p/ /b/			/t/ /d/		/k/ /g/	
Fricatives		/f/ /v/	/th/ /<u>th</u>/	/s/ /z/	/sh/ /zh/		/h/[1]
Affricatives					/ch/ /j/		
Nasals	/m/			/n/		/ng/	
Lateral				/l/			
Semivowels	/ʰw/ /w/[2]			/r/	/y/		

Type of Consonant Sound

1 Classed as a fricative on the basis of acoustic effect. It is like a vowel without voice.

2 /ʰw/ and /w/ are velar as well as bilabial, as the back of the tongue is raised as it is for /u/.

Adapted with permission from Bolinger, D. 1975. *Aspects of Language* (2nd ed.). Harcourt Brace Jovanovich, p. 41.

English Vowel Chart

English Vowel Chart

ē
1. me
2. these
3. see
4. eat
5. chief
6. happy
7. key
8. either

ĭ
1. sit
2. gym

ā
1. baby
2. make
3. rain
4. play
5. eight
6. vein
7. they
8. great
9. straight

ĕ
1. pet
2. head

ă
1. cat

ī
1. item
2. time
3. pie
4. my
5. right

ǝ
1. about
2. lesson
3. elect
4. definition
5. circus

ŏ
1. fox
2. swap

ŭ
1. cup
2. cover
3. flood
4. tough
5. among

aw
1. saw
2. pause
3. call
4. dog
5. wall

ō
1. go
2. vote
3. boat
4. show
5. toe

o͞o
1. moo
2. ruby
3. tube
4. chew
5. blue
6. suit
7. soup

o͝o
1. took
2. put
3. could

er
her
fur
sir

ar
cart

or
sport

oi	oy
oil	boy

ou	ow
out	cow

Note: The order of spelling examples reflects the relative frequency of incidence for that spelling of the phoneme.

Vowel Chart based on Moats, L.C. (2003). *LETRS: Language Essentials for Teachers of Reading and Spelling,* Module 2 (p. 98). Adapted with permission of the author. All rights reserved. Published by Sopris West Educational Services.

Consonants

p	pup, rapped, pie	zh	vision, treasure, azure
b	bob, ebb, brother	h	hat, here, hope
t	tire, jumped, hurt	ch	church, match, beach
d	deed, mad, filed	j	judge, enjoy, jell
k	cat, kick, cut	m	mop
g	get, gill, magazine	n	not
f	fluff, rough, photo	ng	sing
v	valve, every, eleven	l	land
th	thin, three, math		
th	this, there, mother	w	with, wagon, west
s	sod, city, list	r	ramp
z	zebra, has, bees	y	yard, yes, yellow
sh	ship, sugar, machine		

Vowels

ē	beet	(bēt)	ō	boat	(bōt)
ĭ	bit	(bĭt)	o͝o	put	(po͝ot)
ā	bait	(bāt)	o͞o	boot	(bo͞ot)
ĕ	bet	(bĕt)	oi	boil	(boil)
ă	bat	(băt)	ou	pout	(pout)
ī	bite	(bīt)	î	peer	(pîr)
ŏ	pot	(pŏt)	â	bear	(bâr)
ô	bought	(bôt)	ä	par	(pär)
ŭ	but	(bŭt)	ô	bore	(bôr)
ə	rabbit	(ră' bət)	û	pearl	(pûrl)

about	bath	branches	cash	cliff
act	bathtub	brand	cast	cling
ale	bed	brass	catch	clock
all	been	brave	catfish	close
almost	beg	bred	catsup	cloth
alone	bell	bride	cave	club
already	belt	bring	cave-in	clump
also	bench	brink	chant	clung
although	bend	broke	chap	code
always	bent	broth	chase	coke
annex	best	brush	chat	come
any	bet	buck	check	cone
anybody	bike	bud	checkup	context
anyhow	bite	bug	chess	cope
anyone	black	bulb	chest	cost
anything	blacksmith	bulk	chestnut	could
anytime	blade	bull	chick	cove
anyway	blame	bulldog	chill	crab
anywhere	blank	bump	chime	crack
ape	blaze	bun	chimp	craft
ash	bled	bunch	chin	crane
ask	blend	bunk	chip	crank
aspect	bless	bus	chipmunk	crash
asset	blink	bush	choke	crate
ate	block	bust	chop	credit
backhand	bluff	but	chose	crept
backstretch	blunt	butt	chuck	crest
bake	blush	buzz	chum	crime
bale	body	cake	chunk	crops
band	bond	call	clam	cross
bang	bone	came	clang	crude
bank	bones	camp	clash	crunch
base	brake	cane	class	crush
batch	branch	case	click	crust

crutch	dress	evening	fled	gland
cub	drift	every	flesh	glass
cull	drink	exact	flex	glen
cult	drive	exam	fling	glimpse
cup	drop	exist	fluff	glove
cusp	drove	exit	flung	gong
cut	drug	exotic	flunk	got
cutback	drum	expect	flush	grade
cute	drunk	express	flute	grant
dash	duck	fact	flux	grape
date	duct	fade	fond	grasp
daze	dud	fake	forget	grass
deck	dude	fame	frame	grave
den	dug	fast	frank	gremlin
dense	dugout	fate	fresh	grid
dent	duke	faze	frog	grim
depth	dull	fed	from	grime
desk	dump	fell	front	gripe
desktop	dusk	felt	froze	grove
dime	dust	fetch	full	grub
dine	dwell	fifth	fullback	gruff
discuss	each	file	fume	grunt
disgust	ebb	filled	fun	gull
dish	edit	filth	fund	gulp
disk	egg	find	fuss	gum
dispel	eggnog	fine	gale	gun
disrupt	eggplant	finished	game	gust
ditch	eggs	fish	gang	gut
dive	elk	fist	gash	hale
dome	else	five	gate	hand
done	end	flake	gave	handout
dove	epic	flame	gaze	handspring
Dr.	ethic	flash	get	hang
draft	ethnic	flat	glad	hatch
drank	eve	fleck	glade	hate

haze	ink	lash	made	much
hectic	input	last	make	mud
held	insect	latch	male	muffin
help	insects	late	mane	mug
hem	inspect	led	many	mule
hen	instep	left	mash	mum
hide	instruct	leg	mast	mumps
hike	intend	legging	match	mush
himself	into	legs	mate	must
hint	invest	lend	math	mustang
hitch	itch	length	maze	mute
hive	jade	lens	melt	mutt
hole	jell	lent	men	name
home	jest	less	mend	neck
honk	jet	let	mesh	nest
hope	jilt	letdown	mess	net
hose	jive	life	met	next
huff	joke	lifted	metric	nine
hug	jug	liftoff	mile	none
hull	jump	like	milk	nose
hum	jumped	lime	mime	notch
humbug	junk	limp	mine	note
hump	just	line	mink	nothing
hunch	jute	lineup	misled	nut
hunchback	kept	link	misspell	o'clock
hung	killed	list	mist	off-line
hunk	kilt	live	mode	offset
hunt	king	lobe	mole	offspring
hunting	kite	lone	monk	once
hush	know	long	month	one
hut	lake	love	months	oneself
inch	lame	luck	moth	online
inches	land	lump	Mr.	only
income	lane	lunch	Mrs.	our
index	lapse	lung	Ms.	out

outbid	pink	pulled	rise	scrub
outcast	pipe	pulp	rite	scum
outcome	pitch	pulpit	robe	sect
outdid	plan	pulse	rode	self
outdo	plane	pump	role	sell
outdoes	plank	pun	rope	send
outdone	plant	punch	rose	sendoff
outfit	plate	punk	rote	sense
outlast	plot	pup	rub	sent
outlet	pluck	push	rude	septic
outside	plug	pushed	ruff	set
pale	plum	put	rug	setup
pane	plume	putt	rule	sextet
passed	plump	quake	rump	shack
past	plus	quench	run	shade
paste	poke	quest	rung	shaft
patch	pole	quilt	rush	shake
path	polish	quite	rust	shale
pave	pond	quote	rustic	shall
peck	pope	rake	safe	shame
peg	pose	ranch	sake	shamrock
pelvic	prep	rang	sale	shape
pelvis	press	rank	same	shave
pen	pride	rash	sand	shed
pent	prime	rate	sandwich	shellfish
pep	printed	rave	sane	shelve
peptic	prize	red	sang	shift
pest	products	rent	sank	shin
pet	prose	rest	sapling	shine
picked	prospect	rich	sash	ship
pickup	public	ride	save	shock
pigpen	publish	ring	scale	shone
pike	puff	rink	scope	shop
pile	pug	rinse	scrap	shot
pinch	pull	ripe	scratch	should

shove	smash	splash	stripe	tank
shrank	smell	split	strode	tape
shrill	smile	spoke	stroke	tell
shrimp	smiled	spot	strong	tempt
shrine	smith	sprang	struck	ten
shrink	smoke	spring	strung	tend
shunt	snake	spun	stub	tennis
shut	snap	staff	stuck	tense
shutout	snatch	stake	stud	tent
side	snide	stale	stuff	tenth
silk	snug	stand	stump	test
sing	soft	standoff	stunt	text
sink	sole	state	submit	than
site	solve	stem	subtract	thank
size	some	stench	such	thankless
skate	somehow	step	suds	that
skeptic	someone	stick	suffix	theft
sketch	something	still	sum	their
skill	somewhat	sting	summit	them
skulk	somewhere	stink	sun	theme
skull	son	stinkbug	sung	themselves
skunk	song	stitch	sunk	then
slang	span	stock	sunlit	these
slash	spank	stole	sunset	thick
slate	speck	stone	swell	thickness
sled	specs	stop	swept	thin
slept	sped	stove	swim	thing
slid	spell	strand	swing	think
slime	spend	strap	swish	this
sling	spendthrift	strength	switch	those
slip	spent	stress	swung	thought
slope	spin	stretched	take	thrift
slug	spine	strict	take care	thrill
slum	spit	string	tale	thrive
small	spite	strip	tame	throng

thrust	trust	vet	while	won
thump	tub	vile	whim	word
thus	tube	vine	whine	would
tide	tug	vote	whip	wove
tile	tune	wade	whiplash	write
time	twin	wake	white	yank
ton	twine	wane	wide	yell
tone	twitch	wave	wife	yelp
too	two	waves	wind	yes
track	twosome	web	wing	yet
trade	until	wed	wings	yoke
trash	up	welcome	wink	yourself
trench	upon	well	wipe	yule
trend	us	went	wish	zest
trespass	use	wept	witch	zone
tribe	vane	west	with	
trip	vase	wet	within	
trite	vent	whale	without	
truck	very	when	withstand	
trunk	vest	which	woke	

The definitions that accompany the readings relate to the context of the readings. They are provided to help students understand the specific reading selection. For complete definitions of these words, consult a dictionary. Pronunciations are taken from *American Heritage® Dictionary of the English Language*, Fourth Edition.

abyss (ə-bĭs')—a huge, bottomless space

adequate (ăd'ĭ-kwĭt)—enough to meet a need

agility (ə-jĭl'ĭ-tē)—the ability to move quickly and skillfully

altitudes (ăl'tĭ-to͞odz')—heights above the earth's surface

antennae (ăn-tĕn'ē)—thread-like feelers on the heads of some animals

astonished (ə-stŏn'ĭsht)—extremely surprised

atoms (ăt'əmz)—the smallest units of an element

automatically (ô'tə-măt'ĭk-lē)—self-operating; working by itself

avid (ăv'ĭd)—eager; enthusiastic

avoid (ə-void')—to stay away from

backed up (băkt' ŭp)—*v.* copied a computer file or program to have a copy of the original

backup (băk'ŭp)—*n.* a copy of a program or file stored separately from the original

band (bănd)—a narrow strip

basic (bā'sĭk)—original; necessary

basis (bā'sĭs)—a starting point

Berlin (bûr-lĭn')—the capital city of Germany

Big Apple (bĭg ăp'əl)—a nickname for New York City

biologists (bī-ŏl'ə-jĭsts')—people who study living things

bustled (bŭs'əld)—swarmed, buzzed

casual (kăzh'o͞o-əl)—relaxed; not formal

catering (kā'tə-rĭng)—preparing and providing food for banquets and parties

certain (sûr'tn)—sure to happen

chef (shĕf)—a person who prepares food; a cook

cold cuts (kōld kŭts)—cold slices of meat

commercial (kə-mûr'shəl)—related to buying and selling goods or services

compete (kəm-pēt')—to be in a contest

comprehend (kŏm'prĭ-hĕnd')—to understand

confirms (kən-fûrmz')—proves; shows to be true

consequences (kŏn'sĭ-kwĕns'ĭz)—effects; results

conservation (kŏn'sûr-vā'shən)—the protection of natural resources such as forests, soil, and water

consider (kən-sĭd'ər)—to think about

continuous (kən-tĭn'yo͞o-əs)—going without stopping

coordinated (kō-ôr'dən-āt'ĭd)—organized to work well together

cues (kyo͞oz)—signals showing when to start an action

culinary (kyo͞o'lə-nĕr'ē)—of or relating to cooking

definite (dĕf'ə-nĭt)—clear; easy to see; specific

diameter (dī-ăm'ĭ-tər)—the width from one side of a circle to the other

digest (dī-jĕst')—to break down food in the stomach

divided (dĭ-vīd'ĭd)—split or separated into sections or parts

dominated (dŏm'ə-nātəd)—controlled; held power over

dress rehearsal (drĕs rĭ-hûr'səl)—the final practice before a performance

Dust Bowl (dŭst bōl)—the period of powerful dust storms that destroyed crops in the midwestern and southern plains in the 1930s

earl (ûrl)—a British position of high social class

eerie (îr'ē)—mysterious and frightening

elastic (ĭ-lăs'tĭk)—capable of being stretched

eluded (ĭ-lood'ĭd)—stayed away from or escaped

emotion (ĭ-mō'shən)—a strong feeling

en route (ŏn root')—on the way

equinox (ē'kwə-nŏks')—the first day of spring or fall, when day and night are equal length

equivalent (ĭ-kwĭv'ə-lənt)—something that is equal to another

excel (ĭk-sĕl')—to do much better than average

expression (ĭk-sprĕsh'ən)—a saying; a particular way of saying things

feat (fēt)—an unusual skill or ability

flexible (flĕk'sə-bəl)—easily bent without breaking

flourishing (flûr'ĭ-shĭng)—succeeding, prospering

fortunately (fôr'chə-nĭt'-lē)—luckily

fragrance (frā'grəns)—a sweet or pleasant smell or scent

Great Depression (grāt dĭ-prĕsh'ən)—a long period of economic slowdown and unemployment during the 1930s

Great Plains (grāt plānz)—the grassland region of central North America extending from Canada to Texas

guidelines (gīd'līnz')—rules

guzzle (gŭz'əl)—to drink very fast

homeland (hōm'lănd)—one's place of birth

hunker (hŭng'kər)—to settle down; to stay put

imaginary (ĭ-măj'ə-nĕr'ē)—not real; not actually existing

impress (ĭm-prĕs')—to please others

ingredients (ĭn-grē'dē-ənts)—food items used in a recipe

instinctively (ĭn-stĭngk'tĭv-lē)—doing something without thinking about it

integral (ĭn-tĕg'rəl)—essential; necessary

interact (ĭn'tər-ăkt')—to give and receive information

Internet (ĭn'tər-nĕt')—a system connecting computers around the world

intertwines (ĭn'tər-twīnz')—combines, mixing parts of each

intricate (ĭn'trĭ-kĭt)—having many parts or details

intrigued (ĭn'trēgd')—fascinated or interested

jade (jād)—a green color

lapping (lăp'ĭng)—gently splashing or slapping against

ligaments (lĭg'ə-mənts)—bands of strong tissue that connect bones or support other body parts

links (lĭngks)—*n.* connecting elements in a communication system *v.* to connect

local (lō'kəl)—nearby, as in the same town

loom (lōōm)—a machine used to combine thread or yarn into cloth

mandolin (măn'də-lĭn)—a high-pitched, stringed musical instrument

maneuverable (mə-nōō'vər-ə-bəl')—can be moved easily

manufacture (măn'yə-făk'chər)—to make large quantities by hand or machine

method (mĕth'əd)—a regular way of doing something

mild (mīld)—not strong tasting

modern (mŏd'ərn)—related to today's life; current

mystics (mĭs'tĭks)—people who study life's mysteries

odd (ŏd)—strange or unusual

optional (ŏp'shə-nəl)—not required; left to one's choice

ordinary (ôr'dən-ĕr'ē)—common; average quality

pause (pôz)—to stop for a moment

permanent (pûr'mə-nənt)—lasting forever

permission (pər-mĭsh'ən)—an approval; the right to

philosophers (fĭ-lŏs'ə-fərz)—people who study life, truth, and knowledge

physicist (fĭz'ĭ-sĭst)—a person who studies matter and energy

pipe band (pīp' bănd)—a group playing bagpipes

plague (plāg)—a huge number of harmful insects

poignant (poin'yənt)—strongly felt; stimulating

poll (pōl)—a way of counting different opinions

practical (prăk'tĭ-kəl)—useful, handy

precious (prĕsh'əs)—extremely valuable; costly

precise (prĭ-sīs')—exact

predators (prĕd'ə-tərz)—living things that kill and eat other living things

predictable (prĭ-dĭkt'ə-bəl')—capable of being figured out ahead of time; expected

preference (prĕf'ər-əns)—a choice; a selection

preserving (prĭ-zûr'vĭng)—maintaining; keeping in good condition

program (prō'grăm)—*n.* 1. a performance 2. a set of coded instructions that tell a computer to perform a task

programmed (prō'grămd')—*v.* set up a machine to perform specific acts

progresses (prō-grĕs'ĭz)—moves ahead; develops

pronunciation (prə-nŭn'sē-ā'shən)—the way of saying a word

property (prŏp'ər-tē)—things or land owned by someone

protagonist (prō-tăg'ə-nĭst)—the main character

protein (prō'tēn')—a natural material found in all living things

radical (răd'ĭ-kəl)—extreme, drastic

random (răn'dəm)—without purpose or plan; by chance

ravaged (răv'ĭjd)—completely destroyed

refers (rĭ-fûrz')—relates to; means

relied (rĭ-līd')—depended on

reveres (rĭ-vîrz')—feels that something is very special; cherishes

revived (rĭ-vīvd')—brought back into use

sacred (sā'krĭd)—religious; holy

scalp (skălp)—the skin on top of the head

sharp (shärp)—strong in odor or taste

solos (sō'lōz)—performances done by one person alone

sorrow (sŏr'ō)—a deep sadness

spectators (spĕk'tā'tərz)—people watching an event

spindles (spĭn'dlz)—rods or pins on which fibers are spun

spread (sprĕd)—*n.* a bed covering *v.* to move over an area

stability (stə-bĭl'ĭ-tē)—strength and security

staple (stā'pəl)—a common, basic food

sterile (stĕr'əl)—completely clean with no germs or bacteria

stunned (stŭnd)—surprised or shocked

subside (səb-sīd')—to return to a normal level

surface (sûr'fəs)—to rise to the top

suspicious (sə-spĭsh'əs)—having doubt

symbol (sĭm'bəl)—a thing that represents something very important or meaningful

system (sĭs'təm)—a group of related parts working together for a common purpose

theories (thē'ə-rēz)—views or opinions that have not yet been proven true

traditional (trə-dĭsh'ə-nəl)—relating to beliefs or customs kept over time

trudged (trŭjd)—walked with difficulty

Ukraine (yōō-krān')—a country in Eastern Europe

unique (yōō-nēk')—one of a kind

unofficial (ŭn'ə-fĭsh'əl)—not valid or certified

vanished (văn'ĭsht)—disappeared quickly

various (vâr'ē-əs)—different kinds

vary (vâr'ē)—to show change

velocity (və-lŏs'ĭ-tē)—speed

vessel (vĕs'əl)—a hollow container, such as a pitcher, used to hold liquids

victim (vĭk'tĭm)—one harmed by another

waned (wānd)—decreased slowly

wealth (wĕlth)—a large amount

weave (wēv)—to cross threads over and under one another to make cloth

zones (zōnz)—areas of land or sky that have a special purpose

Grammar and Usage References

Noun Form and Function (Units 1, 2, 3, 4, 7, 8, and 11)

Form	Function
Adding the suffix **-s** to most singular nouns . . . . makes a plural noun.	
• map + s = maps • cab + s = cabs • mast + s = masts	• I had the **maps** at camp. • The **cabs** are fast. • The bats sat on the **masts**.
Adding the suffix **-es** to nouns ending in **s**, **z**, **x**, **ch**, **sh**, or **tch** . . . . . makes a plural noun.	
• dress + es = dresses • fizz + es = fizzes • box + es = boxes • rich + es = riches • dish + es = dishes • match + es = matches	• Rose bought three new **dresses**. • They drank cherry **fizzes**. • The **boxes** were full of books. • The safe contains many **riches**. • The **dishes** fell to the floor. • The wet **matches** would not light.
Adding the suffix **-'s** to nouns . . . . . makes a possessive singular noun.	
• Stan + 's = Stan's • van + 's = van's • man + 's = man's	• **Stan's** stamps are at camp. • The **van's** mat is flat. • The **man's** plan is to get clams.
Adding the suffix **-s'** to nouns . . . . . makes a possessive plural noun.	
• boy + s' = boys' • girl + s' = girls' • dog + s' = dogs'	• The **boys'** cards were missing. • The **girls'** snacks are on the table. • The **dogs'** bowls are empty.

Verb Form and Function (Units 4, 5, 7, 8, 10, and 11)

Form	Function
Adding the suffix **-s** to most verbs . .	makes the verbs third person singular present tense.
• sit + s = sits • skid + s = skids • pack + s = packs	• The rabbit **sits** in the grass. • The cab **skids** on the ramp. • She **packs** her bags for the trip.
Adding the suffix **-es** to verbs ending in **s**, **z**, **x**, **ch**, **sh**, or **tch**	makes the verbs third person singular present tense.
• press + es = presses • buzz + es = buzzes • wax + es = waxes • switch + es = switches • wish + es = wishes • pitch + es = pitches	• He **presses** the button to open the door. • The bee **buzzes** around the room. • John **waxes** his car once a month. • She **switches** on the radio. • Jamal **wishes** he had a wagon. • Monica **pitches** her trash into the can.
Adding the suffix **-ed** to regular verbs	makes the past tense.
• jump + ed = jumped • smell + ed = smelled • end + ed = ended	• She **jumped**. • Stuart **smelled** the roses. • The class **ended** well.
Adding the word *will* before main verbs	makes the future tense.
• will + nap = will nap • will + send = will send • will + use = will use	• The cat **will nap** in the afternoon. • They **will send** the package later. • Ron **will use** blue paint.

Form	Function
Adding the suffix **-ing** to verbs with the helping verb *am, is,* or *are*	makes the present progressive.
<ul><li>go + ing = going</li><li>come + ing = coming</li><li>drop + ing = dropping</li></ul>	<ul><li>I **am going** to the circus.</li><li>She **is coming** over to visit.</li><li>Leaves **are dropping** from the tree.</li></ul>
Adding the suffix **-ing** to main verbs with helping verbs *was* or *were*	makes the past progressive.
<ul><li>push + ing = pushing</li><li>dump + ing = dumping</li></ul>	<ul><li>He **was pushing** the cart.</li><li>They **were dumping** sand into the water.</li></ul>
Adding the suffix **-ing** to main verbs with helping verbs *will be*	makes the future progressive.
<ul><li>act + ing = acting</li><li>bring + ing = bringing</li><li>swim + ing = swimming</li></ul>	<ul><li>I **will be acting**.</li><li>She **will be bringing**.</li><li>They **will be swimming**.</li></ul>

Spelling Rules (Units 5, 6, and 10)

Form	Function
-ss, -ff, -ll, and **-zz** At the end of one-syllable words, after a short vowel, $/ s /$, $/ f /$, $/ l /$, and $/ z /$ are usually represented by double letters **-ss, -ff, -ll,** and **-zz**.	<ul><li>pa**ss**</li><li>sti**ff**</li><li>wi**ll**</li><li>ja**zz**</li></ul>

Form	Function
The Doubling Rule Double the final consonant before adding a suffix to a word when: • The word is one syllable. • The word has one vowel. • The word ends in one consonant. Examples: • sip + ing = sipping • skid + ed = skidded	 • She **is sipping** milk. • The cabs **skidded** on the damp ramp.
Final Silent <u>e</u>	
When adding a suffix that begins with a **vowel** to a **final silent <u>e</u>** word.	drop the **<u>e</u>** from the base word.
	• hope + ing = **hoping**
When adding a suffix that begins with a **consonant** to a **final silent <u>e</u>** word.	do not drop the **<u>e</u>** from the base word.
	• hope + ful = **hopeful**

Subject Pronouns (Unit 4)

Person	Singular	Plural
First Person	I	we
Second Person	you	you
Third Person	he, she, it	they

The Present Tense (Unit 4)

Person	Singular	Plural
First Person	I pass.	We pass.
Second Person	You pass.	You pass.
Third Person	He, she, it passes.	They pass.

The Past Tense (Unit 7)

Person	Singular	Plural
First Person	I passed.	We passed.
Second Person	You passed.	You passed.
Third Person	He, she, it passed.	They passed.

The Future Tense (Unit 10)

Person	Singular	Plural
First Person	I will pass.	We will pass.
Second Person	You will pass.	You will pass.
Third Person	He, she, it will pass.	They will pass.

The Present Progressive (Unit 5)

Person	Singular	Plural
First Person	I am sitting.	We are sitting.
Second Person	You are sitting.	You are sitting.
Third Person	He, she, it is sitting.	They sit.

The Past Progressive (Unit 9)

Person	Singular	Plural
First Person	I was passing.	We were passing.
Second Person	You were passing.	You were passing.
Third Person	He, she, it was passing.	They were passing.

The Future Progressive (Unit 11)

Person	Singular	Plural
First Person	I will be passing.	We will be passing.
Second Person	You will be passing.	You will be passing.
Third Person	He, she, it will be passing.	They will be passing.

Irregular Past Tense Verbs (Units 1–12)

Base Verb	Irregular Past Tense	Base Verb	Irregular Past Tense
be (am, is, are)	was/were	ring	rang
bend	bent	rise	rose
bring	brought	run	ran
catch	caught	say	said
come	came	sell	sold
cost	cost	send	sent
cut	cut	shake	shook
dive	dove	shine	shone
do	did	sing	sang
drink	drank	sit	sat
drive	drove	spend	spent
fit	fit	spring	sprang
forget	forgot	stand	stood
get	got	stick	stuck
give	gave	string	strung
go	went	swim	swam
have	had	swing	swung
hit	hit	take	took
know	knew	think	thought
lend	lent	thrust	thrust
let	let	wake	woke
make	made	win	won
put	put	withstand	withstood
ride	rode	write	wrote

Prepositions (Unit 4)

about	as	by	into	since
above	at	down	like	than
across	before	during	near	to
after	behind	except	of	toward
against	below	for	off	under
along	beside	from	on	until
among	between	in	over	up
around	beyond	inside	past	with

Idioms (Units 4–12)

Idiom	Meaning
at the drop of a hat	immediately and without urging
be all wet	be entirely mistaken
be at the end of your rope	be at the limit of one's patience, endurance, or resources
be in full swing	be at the highest level of activity
be in the red	be operating at a loss; in debt
be in the swim	active in the general current of affairs
be in the wind	likely to occur; in the offing
be on the blink	be out of working order
be on the rack	be under great stress
be on to	be aware of or have information about
be on your last leg	be unable to continue
be out of line	be uncalled for; improper; out of control
be out of your hands	be no longer within your responsibility or in your care
be out to lunch	not be in touch with the real world
be over the hump	be past the worst or most difficult part or stage
be up a creek	be in a difficult situation
be within an inch of	be almost to the point of
bite the dust	fall dead, especially in combat; be defeated; come to an end
call it quits	stop working or trying
call the shots	exercise authority; be in charge
call your bluff	challenge another with a display of strength or confidence
catch red-handed	catch someone in the act of doing something wrong
catch you in the act	catch you doing something illegal or private
come to life	become excited
come up smelling like a rose	result favorably or successfully
do the trick	bring about the desired result
fill the bill	serve a particular purpose

Idioms

Idiom	Meaning
don't bug me	leave me alone
get down to brass tacks	begin talking about important things; get down to business
get it off your chest	let go of your pent-up feelings
get off your back	have someone stop bothering you
get on the stick	begin to work
get ripped off	be taken advantage of
get the ax	get fired
get up on the wrong side of bed	be in a really bad mood
give it your best shot	try as hard as you can to accomplish something
go down the tubes	fall into a state of failure or ruin
go to bat for	give help to; defend
go up in smoke	be totally destroyed
have a bone to pick	have grounds for a complaint or dispute
have a leg to stand on	have a good defense for your opinions or actions
have you in stitches	have you laughing uncontrollably
hit close to home	affect your feelings or interests
hit the deck	get out of bed; fall or drop to a prone position; prepare for action
hit the jackpot	win; have success
hit the sack	go to bed
hit the spot	be exactly right; be refreshing
kick the habit	free oneself from addiction, as cigarettes
lend a hand	help someone
let the cat out of the bag	let a secret be known
make a dent in	get started with a series of chores
pass the buck	shift responsibility or blame to another person
pass the hat	take up a collection of money
pat on the back	congratulate; encourage someone
pull a fast one	play a trick or carry out a fraud

Idiom	Meaning
pull your leg	kid, fool, or trick you
push your luck	expect continued good fortune
put all your eggs in one basket	risk everything all at once
ring a bell	arouse an indistinct memory
rub your nose in it	remind you of something unfortunate that has happened
run out of gas	exhaust your energy or enthusiasm
send someone packing	dismiss someone abruptly
shake a leg	hurry
sink or swim	fail or succeed on your own
snap out of it	go back to your normal condition from depression, grief, or self-pity
stack the deck	order things against someone
stick to your ribs	be substantial or filling (used with food)
stick your neck out	take a risk
stuck in a rut	staying in a way of living that never changes
take a hike	leave because your presence is unwanted
take a stand	take an active role in demonstrating your belief in something
take it from the top	start from the beginning
tilt at windmills	confront and engage in conflict with an imagined opponent or threat
(when) push comes to shove	(when) the situation becomes more difficult or matters escalate
wing it	go through a situation or process without any plan

Glossary of Terms

Books A and B contain these terms. Unit numbers where these items first appear follow each definition.

Adjective. A word used to describe a noun. An adjective tells which one, how many, or what kind. A prepositional phrase may also be used as an adjective. Example: *The **quick** team **from the school** won the game.* (Unit 6)

Adverb. A word used to describe a verb, an adjective, or another adverb. An adverb answers the questions when, where, or how. A prepositional phrase may also be used as an adverb. Examples: *He ran **daily**. She hopped **in the grass**. He batted **quickly**.* (Unit 4)

Antonym. A word that means the opposite of another word. Examples: *good/bad; fast/slow; happy/sad.* (Unit 2)

Apostrophe. A punctuation mark used in possessive singular and plural nouns. Examples: *Fran's hat, the boys' cards.* It is also used in contractions. Examples: *isn't, can't.* (Units 2, 7)

Attribute. A characteristic or quality, such as size, part, color, or function. Examples: *She lost the **big** stamp. Fish have **gills**. He has a **green** truck. A clock **tells time**.* (Unit 5)

Base Verb. The form of a verb without any suffixes; the infinitive form without *to*. Examples: *be, help, spell.* (Unit 7)

Comma. A punctuation mark used to signal a pause when reading or writing to clarify meaning. Example: *Due to snow, school was cancelled.* (Unit 5)

Compound word. A word made up of two or more smaller words. Examples: *backdrop, hilltop.* (Unit 3)

Conjunction. A word that joins words, phrases, or clauses in a sentence or two sentences. Example: *and.* (Unit 7)

Consonant. A closed sound that restricts or closes the airflow, using the lips, teeth, or tongue. Letters represent consonant sounds. Examples: <u>m</u>, <u>r</u>, <u>g</u>, <u>w</u>, <u>q</u>. (Unit 1)

Consonant blends. Consonant sound pairs in the same syllable. The consonants are not separated by vowels. Initial blends are letter combinations that represent two different consonant sounds at the beginning of a word. Examples: **bl**ack, **br**im, **sk**ill, **tw**in. Final blends are letter pairs that represent two different consonant sounds at the end of a word. Examples: bu**mp**, se**nd**, la**st**. (Unit 11)

Contraction. Two words combined into one word. Some letters are left out and are replaced by an apostrophe. Examples: *isn't, can't, I'd.* (Unit 7)

Clusters. Three or more consecutive consonants in the same syllable. Examples: <u>scr</u>, <u>spl</u>, <u>spr</u>, <u>str</u>. (Unit 11)

Digraph. Two-letter graphemes that represent one sound. Examples: <u>ch</u>, <u>sh</u>, <u>th</u>. (Unit 8)

Direct object. A noun or pronoun that receives the action of the main verb in the predicate. Answers the question: Who or what received the action? Examples: *Casey hit the **ball**. She dropped the **mitt**.* (Unit 3)

Direct object, compound. Two direct objects joined by a conjunction in a sentence. Example: *The bugs infest **crops and animals**.* (Unit 9)

Doubling rule. A spelling rule in English that says to double a final consonant before adding a suffix beginning with a vowel when: 1) a one-syllable word 2) with one vowel 3) ends in one consonant. Examples: *hopping, robbed.* Also called the **1-1-1** Rule. (Unit 6)

Expository text. Text that provides information and includes a topic. Facts and examples support the topic. Example: "What Is Jazz?" (Unit 5)

Expression. A common way of saying something. An expression is similar to an **idiom**. Example: *all wet = mistaken; on the wrong track.* (Unit 7)

Homophones. Words that sound the same but have different meanings. Examples: *son/sun; some/sum; one/won.* (Unit 7)

Idiom. A common phrase that cannot be understood by the meanings of its separate words—only by the entire phrase. Example: at the drop of a hat = immediately and without urging. (Unit 4)

Narrative text. Text that tells a story. A story has characters, settings, events, and a resolution. Example: "Atlas: The Book of Maps." (Unit 2)

Noun. A word that names a person, place, thing, or idea. Examples: *teacher, city, bat, peace.* (Unit 1)

Noun, abstract. A word that names an idea or a thought that we cannot see or touch. Examples: *love, Saturday, sports, democracy.* (Unit 3)

Noun, common. A word that names a general person, place, or thing. Examples: *man, city, statue.* (Unit 3)

Noun, concrete. A word that names a person, place, or thing that we can see or touch. Examples: *teacher, city, pencil.* (Unit 3)

Noun, proper. A word that names a specific person, place, or thing. Examples: *Mr. West, Boston, Statue of Liberty*. (Unit 3)

Phrase. A group of words that does the same job as a single word. Examples: *at lunch, in the park, to stay in shape*. (Unit 4)

Plural. A term that means more than one. In English, nouns are made plural by adding -**s** or -**es**. Examples: *figs, backpacks, dresses*. (Unit 1)

Possession, singular. One person or thing that owns something. Adding **'s** to a word signals singular possession. Examples: *the man's map, Fran's stamps*. (Unit 2)

Predicate. One of two main parts of an English sentence. It contains the main verb of the sentence. Examples: *He **digs**. She **lost the big stamp***. (Unit 2)

Predicate, simple. The verb in a sentence. Example: *The class **clapped** during the song*. (Unit 8)

Predicate, complete. The verb and all of its modifiers. Example: *The class **clapped during the song***. (Unit 8)

Predicate, compound. Two or more verbs joined by a conjunction. Example: *The class **sang and clapped***. (Unit 8)

Preposition. An English function word that begins a prepositional phrase. Examples: *at, in, from*. (Unit 4)

Prepositional phrase. A phrase that begins with a preposition and ends with a noun or a pronoun. A prepositional phrase is used either as an adjective or as an adverb. Examples: *at the track, in traffic, from the old map*. (Unit 4)

Progressive. A verb form that indicates ongoing action in time. Examples: *I **am going** (present); I **was going** (past); I **will be going** (future)*. (Units 5, 9, 11)

Pronoun. A function word used in place of a noun. Pronouns can be nominative, objective, or possessive. (Units 4, 6, 7)

Pronoun, nominative. A pronoun that takes the place of the subject in a sentence. Also called a subject pronoun. Example: ***He** ran down the street*. (Unit 7)

Pronoun, objective. A pronoun that takes the place of the object in a sentence. Example: *Jason threw **it***. (Unit 7)

Pronoun, possessive. A pronoun that shows possession. Example: *Mary's desk is neat. **Mine** is messy*. (Unit 7)

Sentence. A group of words that has a subject and a predicate. A sentence conveys a complete thought. Examples: *It kicks. The map is in the cab.* (Unit 1)

Sentence, simple. A group of words that has one subject and one predicate. Examples: *The man ran. The plan is abstract.* (Unit 2)

Statement. A sentence that presents a fact or opinion. Examples: *The map is flat. The twins are remarkable.* (Unit 2)

Story. An account of events. A story has characters, setting, events, and a resolution. Example: "Floki, Sailor Without a Map." (Unit 2)

Subject. One of two main parts of an English sentence. The subject names the person, place, or thing that the sentence is about. Examples: ***She** raps. **Boston** digs.* (Unit 2)

Subject, complete. A subject (noun or pronoun) and all of its modifiers. Example: ***The blue egg** fell from the nest.* (Unit 7)

Subject, compound. A subject that consists of more than one noun or pronoun joined by a conjunction. Example: ***Ellen and her class** passed.* (Unit 7)

Syllable. A word or word part that has one vowel sound. Examples: *bat, dig, tox-ic, pic-nic.* (Unit 3)

Synonym. A word that has the same or a similar meaning to another word. Examples: *big/huge, quick/fast, fix/repair.* (Unit 3)

Tense. Changes in the form of a verb that show changes in time: present, past, or future. (Units 4, 7, 10)

Trigraph. A three-letter grapheme that represents one sound. Example: -**tch** (watch). (Unit 8)

Verb. A word that describes an action (*run, make*) or a state of being (*is, were*) and shows time. Examples: *acts* (present tense; happening now), *is dropping* (present progressive; ongoing action), *acted* (past tense; happened in the past), *will act* (future tense; will happen in the future). (Units 4, 5, 7, 10)

Vowel. An open sound that keeps the airflow open. Letters represent vowel sounds. Examples: **a**, **e**, **i**, **o**, **u**, and sometimes **y**. (Unit 1)

Unit 7

Spider Woman

Leet, Karen M. 1996. "Spider Woman," from *Faces* (October), vol. 13, no. 2. Carus Publishing Company, 315 Fifth Street, Peru, IL 61354. All rights reserved. Reprinted with permission.

The Spider's Thread

Ryunosuke, Akutagawa. 1996. "The Spider's Thread: A Folktale from Japan," trans. and adapted by Dean Durber, from *Faces* (October), vol. 13, no. 2. Carus Publishing Company, 315 Fifth Street, Peru, IL 61354. All rights reserved. Reprinted with permission.

Super Webs

Miller, Steve. 1997. "Spinning Superstuff," from *Odyssey* (January), vol. 6, no. 1. Carus Publishing Company, 315 Fifth Street, Peru, IL 61354. All rights reserved. Adapted with permission.

Web Wins

Kornblum, Janet. "Teens' top pastime flips from TV to surfing the Web," *The Detroit News*, 26 July 26. http:// www.detnews.com/2003/homelife/0307/ 26/d01-227515.htm

The World on the Web

Boutell.com. 2003. "How Big Is the Internet?" from *Boutell.com: Purveyors of Quality Web Resources*. http://www.boutell.com/newfaq/basic/ big.html (accessed April 1, 2004).

The World Wide Web

Benedikt, Claire. 1995. "Odyssey On Line: Featuring the Do-It Kids," from *Odyssey* (January), vol. 4, no. 1. Carus Publishing Company, 315 Fifth Street, Peru, IL 61354. All rights reserved. Used with permission.

————. 1995. "Odyssey On Line: 'Kids for Space' on the Internet," from *Odyssey* (October), vol. 4, no. 7. Carus Publishing Company, 315 Fifth Street, Peru, IL 61354. All rights reserved. Used with permission.

————. 1995. "Odyssey On Line: Gaining on the Snail," *Odyssey* (April), vol. 4, no. 4. Carus Publishing Company, 315 Fifth Street, Peru, IL 61354. All rights reserved. Used with permission.

Unit 8

Hmong Song

Alliance for California Traditional Arts. "Hmong Qeej Making: Cha Tou Xiong and Vungping Yang." www.actaonline.org/ apprenticeships/2000/xiong_cha_tou.htm (updated 2002).

PBS.org. 1998. "Americans Old and New: Hmong Qeej Players, St. Paul, Minnesota," from *The Mississippi: River of Song*. www.pbs.org/riverofsong/ artists/e1-hmong.html.

PBS.org. 2003. "Hmong Culture: Music," from *The Split Horn: Life of a Hmong Shaman in America*. www.pbs.org/ splithorn/hmong.html.

Sloan, Cliff. 2003. "Hmong Music: Talking Instruments," from *Folk Arts Projects: Asian American Traditional Festivals*. www.arts.wa.gov/progFA/AsianFest/ Hmong/fahmong10.html.

Yang, Lao. 2003. "Hmong Music: The Kheng," Paul and Sheila Wellstone Elementary School Student Showcase. ww2.saturn.stpaul.k12.mn .us/Hmong/studentshowcase/reports/ hmongmusic.html (accessed December 2003).

The Power of Song

Black, Bob. 1992. "The Power of Music," from *Faces* (December), vol. 9, no. 4. Carus Publishing Company, 315 Fifth Street, Peru, IL 61354. All rights reserved. Adapted with permission.

Whale Songs

ABC Online. "Whale Song," from *Oceans Alive: Whale Dreams*. Adapted with permission of the Australian Broadcasting Corporation. www.abc.net.au/oceans/whale/song.htm.

Cechvala, Meredith. 2001. "Humpback Whale Songs: Theories of Their Function," from the University of Wisconsin Department of Bacteriology website, www.bact.wisc.edu:81/ScienceEd/stories/storyReader$62 (accessed November 2003).

Woody's Song

Hall, Barbara. 2000. "Woody's Music," from *AppleSeeds* (January), vol. 2, no. 5. Carus Publishing Company, 315 Fifth Street, Peru, IL 61354. All rights reserved. Adapted with permission.

Unit 9

How Bugs Bug Us

Info Adventure. 1996. *Amazing Body Science*. Chicago: World Book Inc./Two-Can Publishing. Adapted with permission of Creative Publishing International. Copyright © 1995 by Two-Can Publishing, an imprint of Creative Publishing International. Adapted by permission of Creative Publishing International.

Sear, Dexter. 2002. "Bugbios," from *Insects.org* website. bugbios.com.

New Old Insects

Platt, Gary. 1998. "What Is Amber?" www.gplatt.demon.co.uk/whatis.htm.

Trivedi, Bijal P. 2002. "New Insect Order Found in Southern Africa," from *National Geographic Today* (March 28). news.nationalgeographic.com/news/2002/03/0328_0328_TVstickinsect.html.

Unit 10

Creating the Calendar

Bianchi, Robert S. 1994. "Egypt: The Sky and the Nile," from *Faces* (December), vol. 11, no. 4. Carus Publishing Company, 315 Fifth Street, Peru, IL 61354. All rights reserved. Adapted with permission.

Kane, Karen. 1994. "China: Sun, Moon, and Animals," from *Faces* (December), vol. 11, no. 4. Carus Publishing Company, 315 Fifth Street, Peru, IL 61354. All rights reserved. Adapted with permission.

Musselman, Kelly. 1999. "Calendar Confusion," from *Odyssey* (December), vol. 8, no. 9. Carus Publishing Company, 315 Fifth Street, Peru, IL 61354. All rights reserved. Adapted with permission.

Stuart, David. 1999. "Maya Writing and the Calendar," from *Calliope* (February), vol. 9, no. 6. Carus Publishing Company, 315 Fifth Street, Peru, IL 61354. All rights reserved. Adapted with permission.

Learning to Tell Time

Cummings and Lucas. 2003. "Clock a History." www.ernie.cummings.net/clock.htm (accessed November 2003).

University of Wisconsin Board of Regents. 1998. "It's About Time" timeline, from *The Why Files*. whyfiles.org/078time/3.html (accessed November 2003).

Sources

The Time Machine

Martin, Les. 1990. Adapted from *The Time Machine* by H. G. Wells, adapted by Les Martin, copyright ©1990 by Random House, Inc. Used by permission of Random House Children's Books, a division of Random House, Inc.

Time Zones

Greenwich Mean Time Homepage, wwp.greenwichmeantime.com/home.htm (accessed Oct. 28, 2003).

Llewellyn, Claire, A. Phillips, and L. Norton. 1995. "Clock," from *Scholastic First Encyclopedia: How Things Work.* New York: Scholastic Publications Ltd.

Unit 11

Hurricane!

Blohm, Craig E. 1986. "Nature's Violent Side," from *Cobblestone* (April), vol. 7, no. 4. Carus Publishing Company, 315 Fifth Street, Peru, IL 61354. All rights reserved. Used with permission.

Dineen, Jacqueline. 2002. *Natural Disasters: Hurricanes and Typhoons.* London: Aladdin Books Ltd. (Permission?)

NOAA: National Weather Service. 2002. "Saffir-Simpson Hurricane Scale," from *Hurricane Awareness.* www.nhc.noaa.gov/HAW2/english/basics/saffir_simpson.shtml.

Wood, Jenny. 1990. *Storms: Facts, Stories, Activities.* Chanhassen, MN: Two-Can Publishing Ltd. Copyright © 1990 by Two-Can Publishing, an imprint of Creative Publishing International. Adapted by permission of Creative Publishing International.

A Kite's Tale

Higbee, Rebecca. 1994. "A Kite's Tale," from *Odyssey* (April), vol. 3, no. 4. Carus Publishing Company, 315 Fifth Street, Peru, IL 61354. All rights reserved. Adapted with permission.

The Dust Bowl

Living in the Dust Bowl. Roop, Peter. 1983. "Living in the Dust Bowl," from *Cobblestone* (December), vol. 4, no. 12. Carus Publishing Company, 315 Fifth Street, Peru, IL 61354. All rights reserved. Used with permission.

Wind Sports

Wind Sports. Kitewing. 2002. From the *Skywings Ltd.* website. www.kitewing.com (accessed Oct. 23, 2003).

Wikipedia, the free encyclopedia. en.wikipedia.org/wiki/Hang_gliding (accessed Oct. 23, 2003).

Willswing.com. 2002. "History of Hang Gliding," from the *Wills Wing Inc.* website. www.willswing.com/articles/history.asp (accessed Oct. 23, 2003). Hang gliding section adapted with permission.

Windsurfer.com. "Everything You Wanted to Know About Windsurfing: A Beginner's Guide," from the *Windsurfing Sports Inc.* website. www.windsurfer.com/beginners/history.html (accessed Oct. 28, 2003).

Unit 12

Eponymous Sandwiches

Jones, Charlotte Foltz. 1991. *Mistakes That Worked: 40 Familiar Inventions and How They Came to Be.* New York: Doubleday.

Terban, Marvin. 1988. *Guppies in Tuxedos: Funny Eponyms*. New York: Clarion Books.

How to Make a Hero Sandwich

Claiborne, Craig. 1985. *Craig Claiborne's The New York Times Food Encyclopedia*. New York: Times Books.

Disney Online. "Food for Father's Day: A Hero Sandwich," from *FamilyFun* online magazine. familyfun.go.com/crafts/season/feature/famf67fathersday/famf67fathersday2.html.

Mariani, John. 1991. *America Eats Out*. New York: Morrow.

———. 1999. *Encyclopedia of Food and Drink*. New York: Lebhar-Friedman.

Morris County Library. 2000. "The Food Timeline: International Cuisine." www.gti.net/mocolib1/kid/foodfaq6.html #quesadillas.

Sandwiches + Hero = Success

Denton, Patti. "Deli Owner Focuses on Healthful Cuisine," February 18, 2004. (accessed August 2, 2004). advancement.sdsu.edu/marcomm/news/clips/Archive/2004/Feb2004/021804/021804cuisine.html.

Kenley, C. "For the Community: Ordinary Women, Extraordinary Thing," June 2002. (accessed August 2, 2004). www.indianapoliswoman.com/myhtml/featurestories/2002july.html.

A World of Sandwiches

Davidson, Alan. 1999. *The Oxford Companion to Food*. New York: Oxford University Press.

Garbaccia, Donna R. 1998. "History of the Bagel," excerpt from *We Are What We Eat: Ethnic Food and the Making of Americans*. New Haven, CT: Harvard University Press (accessed at www.hup.harvard.edu/features/gabwea/bagel.html).

Hall, Cyndy. 1999. "Pass the Bread, Please!" from *AppleSeeds* (February), vol. 1, no. 6. Carus Publishing Company, 315 Fifth Street, Peru, IL 61354. All rights reserved. Adapted with permission.

Kowalski, Kathiann M.. 2002. "More and More 'Mainstream': Arab American Food," from *Cobblestone* (May), vol. 23, no. 5. Carus Publishing Company, 315 Fifth Street, Peru, IL 61354. All rights reserved. Used with permission.

Ottawa Bagel Shop and Deli website. 1999. "A Brief History of Bagels." www.bagelshop.on.ca/history/history.html.

Parkinson, Rhonda. "Dim Sum: Chinese Brunch," from *About.com*. chinesefood.about.com/gi/dynamic/offsit e.htm?site=%2Flibrary%2Fweekly%2Faa 070700a.htm (accessed Oct. 28, 2003).

Valentine, Nancy J. 2000. "A Taste of China," from *AppleSeeds* (April), vol. 2, no. 8. Carus Publishing Company, 315 Fifth Street, Peru, IL 61354. All rights reserved. Adapted with permission.

Photo and Illustration Credits

Cover

Illustration

©Martin French/Morgan Gaynin Inc.

Unit 7

Photographs

1: ©William Ervin/Science Photo Library. 21: Courtesy of NASA. 27: ©William Ervin/Science Photo Library, *inset* ©Royalty Free/Corbis. 28: ©Pascal Goetcheluck/Science Photo Library. 35: Courtesy of John Crossley. 36: ©Marilyn "Angel" Wynn/www.nativestock.com.

Illustrations

16–19: Steve Clark. 20: ©Comstock Images. 30, 32: Stephanie Law.

Unit 8

Photographs

37: ©Harlem Girls Choir 52: ©Royalty Free/Corbis. 53: ©1999-2003 Getty Images. 54–55: *bkd.* ©Morey Mibradt/ Brand X Pictures/PictureQuest. 55: *front* ©Bettmann/Corbis, *bk.* ©Siede Preis/ Photodisc/PictureQuest. 56: ©Masa Ushioda/Seapics.com. 58: Courtesy of National Oceanic and Atmospheric Administration/ Department of Commerce. 60: ©PictureQuest. 61: ©Frank Driggs/ Archive Photos/PictureQuest. 62: ©Neal Preston/Corbis. 63: Courtesy of Hmong Cultural Center St. Paul Minnesota (www.hmongcenter.org). 64: Courtesy of Hmong Cultural Center St. Paul Minnesota (www.hmongcenter.org). 65: Courtesy of Hmong Cultural Center St. Paul Minnesota (www.hmongcenter.org). 66: *t.* Courtesy of The Corries (Music) Ltd. *m.* ©Royalty Free/Corbis. *b.* Royalty Free ©Photodisc. 67: *t.* Royalty Free

©Photodisc. *b.* ©Matthew Impey/ Colorsport/Corbis.

Illustrations

63: Courtesy of Tom Riddle. 64: Courtesy of Nhon Nguyen.

Unit 9

Photographs

69: Royalty Free ©Digital Vision. 85: ©Bio Photo Associates/Science Source. 87: Royalty Free ©Digital Vision. 88: *l.* Royalty Free ©Digital Vision, *r.* Royalty Free ©PhotoDisc. 89: *t.* ©Photo Researchers Inc. *m.* ©PhotoDisc. *b.* ©Andrew Syred/Photo Researchers Inc. 90: Courtesy of Oliver Zompro. 91: Courtesy of Simon van Noort (Iziko Museums of Cape Town). 97: Royalty Free ©Photodisc. 99: Royalty Free ©Photodisc. 100: Royalty Free ©Photodisc.

Illustrations

84: ©1996-2004 Jupiter Images. 85–88, 93, 95–96: Steve Clark.

Unit 10

Photographs

119: ©Artville, ©Comstock Klips. 123: Courtesy of National Institute of Standards and Technology. 125: Sopris West employee watch. 134: ©University of Illinois Library, Rare Books and Special Collections Library, Urbana-Champaign campus. 135: "The Time Machine" © 1960 Turner Entertainment Co. A Warner Bros. Entertainmnet Company. All Rights Reserved.

Illustrations

105: ©Picturequest LLC 1998-2003. 119: *b.* Becky Malone. 120: *b.* ©Picturequest

LLC 1998-2003. 121: ©Picturequest LLC 1998-2003. 124: ©Digital Vision Ltd. 126: Beth Stover/Carus Publishing. 127: Becky Malone. 129: ©Dover Publications 2002. 130: ©1996-2004 Jupiter Images. 131: Used by permission from Prometheus Imports. 133: Courtesy of Danny Cardle. 137–138: Steve Clark.

Unit 11

Photographs

154: ©1999-2003 Getty Images. 157: ©1999-2003 Getty Images. 159: Public Domain. 161: Courtesy of National Oceanic and Atmospheric Administration/ Department of Commerce. 162: Courtesy of Minnesota Historical Society. 164: Library of Congress, Prints and Photograph Division [LC-USF34-009058-C(P&P)]. 165: Courtesy of US National Archives.

166: ©Kai's Power Photos. 168: ©Clay Rogers/Photo Resource Hawaii. 170: ©2002-2004 Veer Inc. 171: Royalty Free/ Corbis.

Illustrations

139: Martin French. 152–153: Steve Clark. 155: ©North Wind Picture Archives.

Unit 12

Photographs

188: ©Photodisc. 189: ©Artville. 193: *t.* ©Stewart Cohen/Getty Images, *b.* National Portrait Gallery, London. 195: ©Corel Royalty Free. 196–197 ©Shawn Spence Photography.

Illustrations

173, 190–191: Steve Clark. 194: ©Liquid Library. 199–201: Steve Clark.